125 Fun Things to Do in Retirement

Bucket List Ideas—The Fun and Adventures of Not Working

Pam Martin

acknowledge that the author is not engaged in the rendering of legal, financial, medical, or professional advice. The content within this book has been derived from various sources. Please consult a licensed professional before attempting any techniques outlined in this book.

By reading this document, the reader agrees that under no circumstances is the author responsible for any losses, direct or indirect, that are incurred as a result of the use of the information contained within this document, including, but not limited to, errors, omissions, or inaccuracies.

Table of Contents

CHAPTER 7: NURTURING YOUR SPIRITUAL SELF AND PERSONAL DEVELOPMENT 67

CHAPTER 8: GIVING BACK THROUGH CHARITY AND VOLUNTEERING 77

Introduction

Retirement is a word that conjures images of relaxation, lazy days, peace, and freedom. When a person retires, they may have a well-thought-out plan for the days ahead. Others may have thousands of ideas, but not know where to start while some retirees will face their upcoming retirement with trepidation, fearing boredom. Inevitably, everyone will reach that time in their working life when they progress to that next phase.

When contemplating retirement, I wondered what I would do after 30 years of being very busy juggling raising kids, managing a career, and all the other things that daily life throws at us. I enjoyed being busy, so the thought of long-term relaxation was a bit daunting for me. I took the retirement plunge after a bit of self-reflection about what I really wanted and enjoyed doing. While creating my own bucket list, visiting all the National Parks in the US was at the top. With research and planning, a year-long epic trip to all the National Parks kickstarted my post-career life.

Enter *125 Fun Things to Do in Retirement: Bucket List Ideas—The Fun and Adventures of Not Working*. If you are looking for ideas for fun and adventurous activities and inspiration, I've got you covered. The items are numbered to ensure you receive what is promised from the title, as well as to encourage you to continue adding items on your own. There is no required order or frequency for the activities either.

In this book, I share my experiences, adventures, and bucket list ideas to inspire and encourage readers to step out of their comfort zone and explore the world around them. From line dancing (#15) to geocaching (#38) to skydiving (#100), this book is packed with ideas for every type of adventurer. I understand that retirement can be a time of anxiety and uncertainty, and my goal is to ease those fears by providing readers with inspiration, variety, and new experiences. I wrote this book with the post-pandemic retiree in mind. The focus is on the variety of experiences available to you, but does not address the step-by-step how-tos for the activities, nor specific planning, financial aspects, or intimate/sexual topics.

This book is more than just a list of activities though. It's a roadmap to living a fulfilling life in retirement. Your preference may lie with interests outside of traveling and physically demanding activities. The majority of today's retirees are Baby Boomers—those born between 1946 and 1964—with varying levels of physical mobility and financial stability. For that reason, the first couple of chapters provide essential activities for entering into retirement mode, being sure to stay physically, mentally, and socially fit. From there, we will look at the wealth of travel opportunities, before delving into education, self-development, and charitable endeavors. Throughout this journey, I discovered that how I spend my retirement is mine for the making and doesn't have to be a time to slow down. Instead, it can be a time of growth, discovery, and adventure. I want each of you, my reader, to view retirement as the start of a new and exciting chapter in your life

So, whether you're looking to explore the great outdoors, try a new hobby, or simply relax and unwind, this book has something for everyone. And who knows? You may just discover your next great adventure.

Chapter 1:

Staying Physically Active

I think one of the hardest things to get used to at the start of my retirement was not having to set an alarm. I didn't *have* to get up at a certain time every morning. I could wear what I wanted, go where I wanted to, when and if I chose. Not just for a week or two vacation. This was my life going forward.

The absence of a schedule can tempt even the most enthusiastic retiree to become lethargic. For this reason, our journey starts with ways to stay physically active. It doesn't matter whether you are a fitness enthusiast or the type of individual who's just looking to keep the muscles limber. If your plan is to travel, you may also want to build your stamina for the physical demands of navigating airports and your other chosen transportation methods. Now is the perfect time to introduce some inspiring ideas that will help you keep moving, stay fit, and feel energized.

Ideas to Keep Moving

In this chapter, we will discuss different physical

activities that you may already be doing. The best thing about retirement is that we can devote more time to the activities we enjoy. Let's look at some of the options to keep you mobile from day one of your retirement life.

1. Walk the Block

Walking is such an underrated activity. It is free, can be done by everyone at any age, and under any conditions. At first, you may need to set a reminder to get mobile, but soon it will become second nature. By yourself or with others. You may be surprised at what else you will notice in your neighborhood as this becomes a habit.

Walking clubs are popular with seniors, primarily for the reasons we mentioned above. First, it's free. You can exercise without having to break the bank. Secondly, you can walk anywhere. If you live near a large shopping mall, there may be a group you can join that does mall walking in inclement weather. Regardless of your location, this is the number one activity to keep you mobile and physically fit.

2. Try Tai Chi

This is an engaging type of martial art that has many benefits including keeping you physically active. The movements in this discipline are designed to focus on strength, flexibility, and balance. As we get older, balance and flexibility are negatively impacted, so spending time daily to strengthen these areas is a must. Join a local tai chi class to learn ways to keep your limbs limber.

Tai chi can be done anywhere. You will often see groups performing the fluid motions in parks and greenspaces. The combination of the rhythmic actions and fresh air serve to enhance the benefits of this activity.

3. Become Flexible With Yoga

Again, the idea here is to maintain flexibility in your muscles. There are various forms of yoga, many of which have been specifically designed for seniors. This way, you aren't going to be subjected to trying out all those difficult poses. Due to the intense focus maintained during the session, this activity provides significant benefits for our mental well-being as well.

One of the most popular versions of yoga for seniors is chair yoga. As we get older, it can be more difficult to get up off the ground without support or assistance. Chair yoga combines the health benefits of yoga positions while seated or using a chair for support.

There are some subtle differences between tai chi and yoga. The former emphasizes continuous movement, while the latter involves working your body into poses which are held for a few seconds at a time. Both activities will help enhance your sense of balance.

4. Dance for Fun and Exercise

Whether in your kitchen moving your body to the latest song on the radio, or out at a club or studio, dancing will undoubtedly make you feel good. There are so many forms of dancing such as salsa, ballroom, hip-hop, and line dancing, just to name a few.

If you are looking to enhance your skills in this area, you can learn from online classes or look up any available ones in your neighborhood senior center or the local community center. There are also many dance studios that offer adult dance classes. Dancing is a great way to merge a love of music with physical activity.

Sports for Competition and Pleasure

Our next series of activities will focus on the most popular sports that many devote their time to in retirement. Although some of the items we will discuss are associated with formal competition, these activities are predominantly recreational. A point to remember is that you don't always have to do things on your own; you can invite a few friends along, or go out with family or your partner and even join a club to enjoy some of your favorite activities.

5. Hit the Golf Course

This activity combines our number one item, walking, with an enjoyable—and often frustrating sport—while enjoying the beautiful outdoors. Depending on where you live, this could be a year round activity.

Golf is an immensely popular sport for retirees. You don't have to wait for the weekend rush to book a tee time either. The added option of using a golf cart to navigate the course can extend your playing days significantly.

6. Go Fishing

It doesn't matter whether it's freshwater or saltwater fishing; just get your rod and lures ready, head to the lake or river, and have some fun. Do you live near the ocean? You might even catch some seafood for your supper.

While fishing isn't necessarily a top sport, it does promote competition between you and the elusive prey. There is minimal cost to this activity, and depending on your location, you can participate year round.

7. Play Tennis

This is another popular sport for seniors. Tennis can be played on a variety of surfaces and either indoors or outside. You can play as a single or with someone else as a doubles player. Your local tennis club can help get you started if you are new to the sport.

You may already be a member of a club, and are excited to use your retirement time to spend more days on the courts. Tennis is a social game as well. Whether family or friends, it is a great way to exercise and have fun.

8. Take Up Table Tennis

Also called ping-pong, many of us likely grew up with a table in our homes. While the level of physicality may seem lower than other sports, don't kid yourself. I have sweated a lot during battles over the table.

This activity can be played anywhere you can set up a table. You can play doubles or singles, or even practice your hand-eye coordination alone with one side of the table up as a backboard. Many community centers and seniors homes have the tables and paddles ready and waiting for you.

9. Play Pickleball

A recent addition to the racquet sport craze is pickleball. Played using a paddle on a modified tennis court, pickleball clubs for those over the age of 55 are springing up across the country.

Pickleball is preferred over tennis by some due to the smaller court size. You are still getting a good workout without the more demanding physical requirements of chasing a tennis ball.

10. Hit the Badminton Birdie

This racquet sport can be played all year round, either indoors or out, depending on your location, although the more formal organizations use indoor courts due to the lightweight shuttlecocks (aka "birdies") used. Anyone who has tried to play a serious outdoor game of badminton knows how the wind plays havoc with the birdies.

The costs associated with setting up a badminton net are limited. Once you have your racquet and birdies you are set to go. Like the other racquet sports, badminton is a social game so whether you are a member of a club, or just enjoying a backyard game with family and friends, you will have fun while exercising.

11. Get a Strike at the Bowling Alley

It's time to get out your bowling shoes, gather a group of friends, and go out to your local bowling alley while enjoying a fun game and knocking down some pins. It's a great way to socialize as well as keep active in a not-so-fast-paced activity. Try both 5-pin and the more challenging 10-pin versions if you are inclined.

If you are a member of a bowling team, now is your time to get in some extra practice. If not, and you are interested in bowling for fitness, find your local bowling alley and investigate your options. For those of you with access, there are also lawn bowling clubs active during the summer months. This is an opportunity to get some fresh air while you exercise.

12. Play Bocce Ball

This fun and strategic game is considered low-impact and is predominantly played outdoors. Originating in Italy, the objective of this game is to throw or roll a colored ball as close as possible to the target ball. This target is much smaller than the balls that you need to roll out.

While similar to lawn bowling in many ways, you don't need a well-manicured facility for bocce ball. This can be played on a beach, a lawn, or anywhere you have a relatively flat surface (though a few bumps can certainly add a challenge in your attempt to hit the target)!

13. Join a Volleyball Team

This is a more physically demanding sport and may not be as popular with the retiree group. There are many formations to use for volleyball so using the six or nine person formation will give you the exercise without the high impact.

The beach version played on the sand can be a lot of fun and less physically taxing. You may also want to consider pool volleyball for a less taxing water version. Either way, there are plenty of options to enjoy this social and physical activity.

14. Take Up Archery

While not as popular as other sports, archery can be an ideal activity to challenge yourself. How close can you shoot your arrow to the center of the target? You aren't expected to get a bullseye every time, but the idea is to aim for the center.

You may have to do some research to find an archery club in your area. As mentioned previously, a great place to start is your local community center or seniors center.

15. Go Swimming

What better way to stay limber than a leisurely swim? Whether it be a dip in the ocean, or indoors in the pool, it will depend on your preference and the climate where you live. Or maybe you are fortunate to have a pool in your backyard.

Swimming is a great activity to help keep legs, knees, and hips limber. There are often senior water aerobics classes that are geared to the level of activity you need. Check with your community pool to see if these classes are offered.

Key Takeaways

In this chapter we discussed the first 15 activities to get us mobile as we commence our retirement life. These are by no means the only physical activities we will discuss in this book, however, each of these activities may be an extension of your interests prior to retiring. The inspiration here is the opportunity to move forward with these activities without necessarily relying on a schedule.

Most of the activities discussed come with the added benefits of being physically active while also meeting new people, discovering new cultures, and expanding your social circle. I hear that tee times at the golf course are less expensive through the week, and there are often senior only times for swimming at pools.

The luxury of being able to participate in your favorite physical activities through the week rather than having to cram all the enjoyment into a weekend is one of the priceless benefits of retirement life. Now that we've had a look at how to keep active, let's move on to the social side of our newfound retirement life.

Chapter 2:

Rekindling or Building

Social Connections

Socialization is an extremely important aspect of our life, regardless of age. This is particularly true for individuals who may have been part of a bustling social environment prior to retirement. Much like physical activity, suddenly finding our social interactions reduced can have a significant impact on our mental health and well-being. This is primarily due to our nature as human beings. We are social creatures who require relationships and the company of others. If we are not socializing with people, we often turn to a pet for love and solace.

Keeping in touch with others and spending time in the company of people in a social setting helps to maintain your emotional and mental health. As you develop connections and interact with others who are maintaining positive relationships, it helps to promote your emotional state and reduce stress while also removing feelings of isolation and loneliness. This can improve your cognitive skills and mental health. You are less likely to develop chronic illnesses when you are mentally happy and you have a strong connection and support from others. The more positive feelings you have, the more positive your outlook on life will be.

In this chapter, we will look at some of the social activities available post-retirement and ways to expand your social circle. There are a lot of people out there looking for others to talk to, have fun with, get advice from, and share activities.

Fun Ideas for Socializing

Here are some ideas that you could try to maintain connections with those who are already in your circle, meet new people, and find those who have the same interests as you.

16. Reconnect With Friends and Family

While this may sound like a lost soul coming in from a desert island, this activity is more about establishing your post-retirement support group. During your busy work life, time for socializing was limited. You now have that opportunity to have a leisurely lunch with a friend or two, or plan a family get-together.

When you are busy with work and family, the extent of our communications may be a quick text of call, and less frequently that we would like. Now that you are retired, you may have other friends who have also recently entered retirement. Catching up over a coffee is no longer a luxury.

17. Join a Local Club or Group

If you are already part of a club or group, now is the time to use every penny of those membership fees! Take the opportunity to participate. If you aren't already a member of a club, and there is one available related to your interest, join it.

There are a variety of clubs or groups, like book clubs, hiking groups, tennis clubs, golf clubs (not the ball-hitting ones, the social ones), and gardening clubs. You can find groups in your area for people who come together for the betterment of society, their neighborhoods, or the environment. It is a great way to combine physical activities with a social setting.

18. Create or Revisit Your Social Media Profile

In this day and age, most of us have an online presence already established on one of the social media platforms. If you haven't done so already, or if your profile needs some updating, now is the time. There are online platforms available for you to join using video chats. Social media platforms are great places to find virtual groups.

Another great feature of being a part of online groups is that you don't have to travel and it is much safer given the context of the recent pandemic. For example, I spent a lot of time on virtual travel sites researching and preparing my itinerary for my National Parks adventure. There are also senior travel groups that provide virtual travel presentations for free. This is a great way to learn about various destinations through knowledgeable travel guides.

19. Attend Events That Interest You

What about attending a concert in the park? Or viewing an exhibit by a favorite artist? What about attending a vintage car rally? Everyone has hobbies or interests that extend to public shows and events. What better time to attend an activity or two (or more) now that you have the time on your hands.

Prior to retiring, you needed to schedule these activities on weekends, which meant higher prices, busier venues, and less availability. Being able to attend such events at your leisure is one of the true benefits of retirement.

20. Join or Create a Community Garden

For those of you with a green thumb, maybe participating in a community garden would be of interest. If your living arrangement does not provide the outdoor space for you to nurture your own garden, a section of a community allotment may be just the thing for your social and growth mindset.

If there isn't a community garden in your neighborhood, then you can get in touch with local authorities, the town council, or the community center, letting them know you would like to get one started and see if there is municipal land available. Once the ball is in motion, get as many people in the community involved as possible for a successful community activity.

21. Host a Theme Dinner

A great way for you to socialize is by hosting things like potluck dinners or murder mystery dinners. Hosting your own party is a good way to bring you closer to your neighbors and friends for a fun and memorable event. If you like the concept and the socializing part but not the preparation and planning, there are a number of organizations that can cater the event for you. Once you begin hosting different events, you will meet a lot of people, and this would be a great chance for you to learn about them and make new friends while having fun.

22. Attend Card Nights or Game Events

These don't have to be special nights anymore, now that you are retired. Get a group together during the day for a round of euchre, bridge, or rummy. I know a number of couples that host monthly card and game events, switching it up each month.

This is a great opportunity to forgo the old standards and try some of the latest board games on the market. A bit of online research can help identify some of the most popular games out there.

23. Explore Opportunities at Senior Centers and Community Centers

Go out and explore the senior citizen community centers in your vicinity for more activities. There are a wealth of resources and group activities available at these locations. Find out more about special classes that they are hosting as well as upcoming social events in your neighborhood.

You will notice throughout this book we often refer to the community and senior centers as a great source of information. What better place to find like-minded people with ideas for enhancing their retirement days. Most of the centers cater to 55+ groups, so you will find social activities that will interest you.

24. Participate in a LARP

LARP stands for Live Action Role Play. While these events can take the form of everything from vampire battles to acting out video games, the most popular versions for adults are the medieval battle and army reenactments. There are specific groups around the world you can join and many host weekend functions or week long gatherings. These events are highly social and you can meet people from all walks of life.

LARP events are fully immersive activities, complete with period costumes. What better way to get involved in these activities than to look and feel the part. While some participants do create their own costumes, there are always costumes available for those new to this activity.

25. Join a Fitness Club or Gym

While it may seem that this activity is better suited in the previous chapter, the social benefits of going to your local gym should not be overlooked. When gyms had to close during the pandemic, many people were able to continue their physical activities in a modified environment, but couldn't wait to get back to the gym because they missed the social aspect.

Your local gyms and fitness studios may also have certain programs and classes designed for seniors. Being able to combine the physical side with the social is a win-win all round. Remember to check with your doctor before undertaking any strenuous exercise routine or classes, just to be on the safe side,

Key Takeaways

Chapter 2 introduced another 10 inspiring activities that focused on the social aspects immediately after retiring. After working for so many years, it would be quite easy just to put your feet up, turn on the television, and be entertained. A day or two of that can admittedly be therapeutic in order to decompress. However, as we discussed in Chapter 1 with maintaining physical mobility, it is imperative that you don't find yourself isolated and lonely. Being alone is okay in the short term, and may be preferred by some. It is all about balancing that with some social stimulation to maintain good mental health.

Becoming part of, or extending, your social circle is more than just a remedy for loneliness. Many of the activities we mention throughout the book benefit from group participation. This is why connecting with local seniors groups and community centers can help enhance your retirement life.

With our physical stamina in check, and having honed our social skills, it's time to put that all to use as we move on to the wonders (wanders?) of travel.

Chapter 3:

Time to Travel

When you reach retirement, one of the first things that comes to mind is seeing the world. You may have already planned a trip or two and are ready to fly or set sail. Everyone has that one special event or festival that they've always dreamed of experiencing. This can be anything from Mardi Gras or Comic-Con to the Rio Carnival, Oktoberfest, Diwali, Holi, the Rioja wine harvest, the Cannes Film Festival, and many more.

Now that you have the time and are not burdened by work or other obligations, you can make a plan to visit one of these special places that host these special events. As we age, we tend to forget that life can be so fun and exciting, and by celebrating a special event or festival with people who are not always of our ethnicity or background, we can experience new things, taste different foods, and learn about the world around us.

In Chapters 1 and 2, I set the stage both physically and socially for your traveling ambitions. By ensuring you have the physical stamina, and a strong social support network, you can venture out safely. Regardless of where you are headed, the whole concept of having that freedom in retirement to go where you want to is exhilarating. Traveling can bring joy and take you to those places from your dreams. After retirement you are bound to look forward to an adventure and this chapter will show you some ways to achieve this.

The Benefits of Traveling

Traveling is not just a getaway for you. It has a number of benefits. These benefits may be spiritual or physical, both of which are essential for your well-being. Here are some of these benefits according to Sauer (2023):

- It helps you open your mind and keep you mentally engaged.

- Traveling can lead to a reduction of stress, minimize heart diseases, and help manage depression by a considerable percentage.

- It helps you become more engaged through the research and planning activities.

- Traveling gives you courage to leave your comfort zone.

- After returning from a vacation your stress levels lower within three or four days.

Let me elaborate a bit more on this in the next section.

26. Plan a Trip

I have included this as one of the 125 activities since the research and planning that goes into taking a trip is in itself inspiring and fun. I've been known to book one trip while planning another, based on a whim and a well-priced flight! When it comes to planning a trip, most of us get excited, while some of us feel overwhelmed. However, things aren't as difficult as they used to be 10 or 20 years ago.

Planning a trip can be extremely exciting because it can be done with a few taps on your laptop keyboard, and you're on your way to your best adventure yet. You can always go to a travel agency and see what offers they have. If you are a member of the automobile association (AAA) for example, their staff will help you with all the resources necessary, whether flying, cruising, or taking a road trip. Your dream vacation might be quite simple to plan with the assistance of a travel agent.

27. Book a Cruise

If you are considering multiple locations—a couple of Caribbean islands for example—think about a cruise in that area. With multiple stops in a relatively short amount of time you can visit a number of islands during one cruise. Cruising is probably one of the most economical methods of travel. You can participate in quite a variety of activities on board your cruise ship as well. Besides swimming pools, there are spas, live shows, casinos, movie theaters, and many more things to do. Some ships even have ice rinks and rock climbing walls for your enjoyment. And there is never a shortage of food or drink, with multiple buffets, restaurants, and coffee shops scattered around the ship.

You can also experience an adventure while cruising as many cruise packages offer excursion activities at each port, like zip-lining or scuba diving. You will also be able to experience exciting culinary items belonging to those specific destinations.

The cruise ship industry was hard hit during the pandemic in 2020, however, as consumer confidence starts to rebound, there are always cruise deals advertised, and may be the more affordable option. Register with *Cruise Critics* to get the latest info on the cruise industry.

28. Rent (or Buy) a Recreation Vehicle (RV)

I know many retirees that opt to sell their home, pack up their belongings in an RV and start touring the country. With your home on wheels, you can plot your route as you see fit. Many campgrounds are quite sophisticated when it comes to RV connections and many even provide restaurants and social events for their guests.

When planning my trip through the national parks, we decided an RV was the way to go. This option allowed us to set our own pace, without having to rush to get to our next hotel booking. In addition, the campsites were right where we wanted to be in the parks.

29. Use Your Travel Points

Knowing that you were headed for retirement, you may have been accumulating points on credit cards or flight credits to use to purchase tickets. Now is the time to look at how best to use those rewards to reduce your travel costs. Maybe you can add a night or two at a hotel, or rent a car with your points.

If you are a member of AAA, or other travel organizations, you may find there are special deals that will provide seasonal and off-season discounts. You have more flexibility in your retirement to schedule your travel when you get the biggest bang for your buck.

30. Take the Train

There are many options for national and international train travel. If you are considering traveling closer to home, check out the train schedules for options. You will get to see all that the views have to offer during the clackety-clack of the train tracks. Many longer train routes offer sleeping cars with berths for families and in room showers. Compact but quite functional.

Many of the mountainous regions have breathtaking views from the scenic train routes. A bit of online research or contact with a travel agent can help you identify these routes. If you are considering travel to Europe, a Eurorail pass is an economical way to travel from region to region.

31. Go Solo

Traveling singles are becoming more and more popular. Tour companies are beginning to understand the negative impact of high single supplements and are gearing tours, accommodations, and activities for those traveling solo. Some cruise lines have sections of the ship geared to solo travelers, with extra safety precautions, lounge areas, and rooms designed for one. If you have dreamed of going somewhere, but are hesitant to travel alone—especially as a female—research the locations and tour operators promoting solo travel.

Many of the senior travel companies include all the costs, such as tips, in their fee, which allows you to budget your travel dollars more effectively. You don't have to worry about having the right currency and denominations at any time. This is all covered by the tour operator.

32. Take a Road Trip

Use your new found freedom to jump in the car and set off across the country. Whether you decide to book activities and accommodations ahead, or just take it day by day, this is a great option for travel enthusiasts. There are a range of options for you and a trip to your local automobile association will certainly assist with planning. Places like AAA help you with recommendations for getting your vehicle ready to travel, best routes to avoid construction, and plenty of ideas of things to see and do on the way.

You may have been thinking about exploring your state, province, or country. Now that you are retired, you have the opportunity to make this dream a reality.

33. Pin the Point on a Map

If you have an adventurous spirit and want to go where the wind blows, try the old pin the tail on the donkey method of choosing your travel destination. Grab a blindfold, a push-pin or two (or more), and a map of the world. If the world map is a bit ambitious for you, set yourself a country or continent boundary, and see where the pinpoint falls!

This is a great way to find a unique starting point for your travels. If you know the vicinity for your travel, the pin may land on a location you normally wouldn't have considered. This is all part of the adventure.

34. Theme Travel

This may sound a bit cryptic, but consider designing your travel plans around a specific theme. As mentioned in the introduction, one of my bucket list travel ideas was to visit all of the National Parks across the country. You may want to visit the birthplace of your 10 favorite authors. Or, like a good friend of mine, plan your travel to include notable cemeteries and crypts. Each to their own, I say!

Having a theme for your travel does help lend a focus to your choice of destinations. You will be able to find routes geared to your theme, with specific points of interest on your way. You may even find accommodations geared to the theme of your choice.

35. Multiple Transportation Travel

Your travel plans do not have to be limited to flying to and from a single destination. Consider a flight to a cruise port, sailing to a new destination, hopping on a train to a cycling enthusiast's dream spot. See how many different modes of transportation you can fit into one vacation. Combining different methods of travel in some situations where you are taking a lot of luggage may be a challenge, but each mode will provide a wealth of opportunities to see the sights and gain new experiences.

Alternatively, you could travel to a base location and span out from there. Rent a car, take a locomotive, find a mule or camel train, or even a Segway to take to uncharted areas. The options are endless.

Key Takeaways

Traveling is one of the activities most synonymous with retirement. Having the freedom and funds to enjoy the world after being tied to a job and career is the goal of many retirees. In this chapter, we looked at various ways to take the travel plunge. As I mentioned, solo travel is becoming more popular, and the variety of senior-led or retiree focused tours has expanded significantly. Most of the tour operators and senior-focused cruise lines offer activities geared to various physical levels and abilities.

Additionally, all-inclusive tours that incorporate not only flights, transportation, and accommodations but meals and all gratuities as well are extremely popular for those wanting to know the overall price up front. A bit of research will lead you to all the answers. Travelling does not have to break your bank. With the proper planning, you can make the most of your travel dollars and make your dreams come true

In the next chapter, we are going to look at how you can devote time to your hobbies and interests during your retirement.

Chapter 4:

Hobbies and Interests

Open up to your creative side and take a journey to enhance or discover your passion. Some of the hobbies and creative ideas listed below may have been a passion of yours once upon a time. Imagine investing the time in something that you enjoy and creating endless and developing those maybe not so hidden talents.

Whether you call it a hobby, a pastime, or an interest, you have something in your life that piques your creative juices. Let's take a look at some of the common and not-so-common ones.

Fun Hobbies and Creative Ideas

There are numerous ideas for being creative and when you create something by yourself it gives you a feeling of achievement and happiness. Taking up new hobbies can be fun and exciting. This section tells you about all the exciting things that are in store for you in the coming days.

36. Try Your Hand at Photography

Photography is a great, creative hobby to develop, as it's an art form that will allow you to capture or even express your perspective on different aspects of the world through your photos. For those looking for a creative outlet, photography is a good option. As you take pictures, you will be able to create stories and memories that will inspire not only you but others as well.

If photography is new to you, and you are lecry about investing in a high tech camera, consider starting out with the features on the camera function available on your smartphone. The technology today is brilliant, including panoramic and portrait options in high definition. It is a good place to start, and I know I always have my phone nearby these days.

37. Take Up Painting

The difference between painting and photography is that the former can be more therapeutic for those who are looking to engage in that artistic practice, which is rewarding. As you paint, you are creating something that has meaning and is beautiful, appearing from your imagination. One of the greatest benefits of painting is that it gives you a way to express yourself.

Here are some of the types of painting mediums:

- Acrylic: This is most suitable for beginners but is also fast-drying.

- Water colors: Watercolors are specially used for their transparency as well as for creating translucent effects. These types of paints are mainly used for delicate subjects or landscapes.

- Oil paints: Oil paints are rich and often resemble butter. It is best for blending or layering.

- Pastels: Pastels are available in different forms: soft pastels, pastel pencils, and oil pastels.

Each of the above options will provide the opportunity to use an array of vibrant colors and textures to complete your masterpiece. You can even paint objects, which may add an intriguing level of fun and complexity to this activity.

38. Discover Geocaching

Geocaching is a modern take on treasure hunting. It is done by using GPS-enabled devices like your smartphone to participate; you need to search for hidden containers, which are called geocaches. The containers are hidden in specific positions or coordinates and it could even be throughout the world.

You will need to create a free account with a geocaching app or website. Then you would need to find geocaches in your area. Using a GPS device or your phone, you can search and navigate to the area where the geocache is located to seek the container. Log your find on the app as well as within the cache container to receive a smiley face icon on the app. This keeps track of your discoveries.

This hobby is for those who love adventure, enjoy playing games, and going on treasure hunts. You can explore new places as you look for hidden treasure; you are active as you walk, hike, or even climb to find your target area. Geocaching stimulates the mind and requires the use of problem-solving skills which is a good exercise for your brain as well as your body.

39. Complete Furniture or Home Restorations

Restoration can apply to anything that needs an update or a return to its original form. From your furniture and fittings to areas of your home, with a bit of research, the proper tools, and patience you can bring these items back to life. When it comes to furniture restoration, this is where you bring life back to old, damaged, or torn-out pieces of furniture. There are things that you could do, which include reupholstering, refinishing, or even repairing damaged items.

You can learn how to do furniture restorations through books or by going to workshops that focus on how to restore old, damaged furniture. You can also find out how to restore furniture through online tutorials. Certain home improvement channels offer TV programs on furniture and home restorations as well. Your local hardware or home improvement store may host workshops and will certainly be able to help you with the materials for your venture.

40. Study Classic Cars

Restoring your classic cars can be extremely rewarding. You may have already completed the restoration and are now attending and/or participating in shows with your beloved vehicles. This is where you bring them back to their former glory by either repairing them, customizing them, or refurbishing them. You can also find an affordable project online, through local auctions, or even at salvage yards. There are resources available, like restoration guides, classic car clubs, and workshops, where you can learn restoration techniques from other car enthusiasts.

41. Dig Into Gardening

For those who pride themselves with having a green thumb or those who just like the opportunity to putter around in a garden. This is a popular pastime for retirees.

Still, many benefits come with gardening. Not only will you be growing something from scratch and making beautiful plants that you could either eat or use for decorating your outdoor and indoor spaces, but they can also be a great source of stress relief as you watch them grow and thrive.

Most people who participate in gardening and horticulture love to speak about how growing their plants helps alleviate daily stress while relaxing their minds. There are also many celebrities who have taken up gardening and have gone through positive changes in their lives.

You can start small with just potted plants and herbs to grow on your windowsill in the kitchen. If you'd like to go even bigger you can start landscaping your front lawn or backyard. Remember that you will need to maintain the garden, so if you are new to this activity, you may want to start with a limited number of plants.

42. Put Pen to Paper and Write

You may already have the writing skills in your arsenal, so retirement is the opportunity for you to expand on your writing or journaling. This is a great way for you to put down your memories and experiences on paper. It is also a creative outlet for you to express yourself. Consider writing your own book as we will discuss further in the next chapter on self-employment, or become a ghostwriter.

There are so many different resources and sources of information that can help you on your writing journey. Online writing communities as well as writing workshops are readily available. Here is the opportunity to use some of the social outlets we discussed in Chapter 2.

Magazines and professional journals are always looking for contributions. Websites and blogs are another good opportunity to capitalize on your writing talents. You can even start your own blog about a topic of interest or share your thoughts on retirement life.

43. Take up Woodworking

Woodworking is a fascinating, detailed art using pieces of timber. You could even use recycled wood for your projects. This is a fun and exciting hobby to have and it is fulfilling to create items from a simple piece of wood. If you live near a beach you can source the material for your word from driftwood.

You can access online resources for tips on how to perform carpentry or woodworking and make items from DIY videos on YouTube. There are various techniques to be used when working with wood, such as burning, or chiseling. There are also books that provide step-by-step information on how to make specific pieces of furniture from scratch if you feel adventurous.

44. Grab the Binoculars and Go Bird-Watching

Another creative hobby to pursue is bird-watching. This is a great way for you to connect with nature as well as to appreciate the beauty of the birds and watch different species communicate and live. The great thing about nature observation aside from the low cost is that there are a wealth of local clubs and groups, like bird-watching clubs, and online communities that share their knowledge. You can participate in events or meetings offered.

Investigate your local wetland or marshland groups for options to check out nesting areas. Due to migratory patterns, you can experience a variety of feathered friends throughout the year.

45. Try Music and Musical Instruments

If you are musically inclined, you probably already have an ongoing relationship with a music group or other organization. In retirement, you can take this a step further by learning a new musical instrument. This is true whether you are trying to get back to playing a certain instrument that you once knew how to play or start fresh.

If your musical talent lies with your vocal ability and you haven't done so previously, now may be the time to join a choir or musical theater group. You could also go online to find tutorials and other music companies to develop your skills and find other seniors who are interested in learning how to make music.

46. Become a Board Game Guru

In Chapter 2, we discussed hosting games or card nights. You may need to expand your horizons about the wealth of challenging options for one or more person activities. You can learn to play a new board game, like chess, and dedicate enough time to it until you become a pro. Or venture beyond the Monopoly board and euchre deck to find the latest trend. Join a games club and who knows, this may lead to a competition down the line.

Have you ever considered designing your own board game? This is an option for retirees looking to enhance their creative side. Maybe a roll of the dice will bring you closer to your new pastime.

47. Read for Pleasure

I'm an avid reader, which helped with my hours and hours of research for this book. However, for enjoyment, I love to sink my teeth into a good crime novel or psychological thriller. Finding a new author is a joy, especially if they have developed a character that has a number of adventures for me to enjoy.

With so many genres available, I know you will find a book or two to spirit you away to another world. Like many of you, I have a stack of unread books in my house on a variety of topics. All of them sitting idly by, waiting for me to have time to open the cover. Retirement is a great time to sit back with a book, without thinking that you really should be doing something else. Just enjoy the moment.

48. Lend a Hand to Environmental Cleanup Projects

The climate and overall destruction of our environment is a concern for all of us. If you are already involved in such groups or events, you know the importance of these activities. Your retirement can afford you the opportunity to get more involved with these organizations.

If you are interested in participating, consider reaching out to a related group in your community. There are a variety of options including fundraising, participating in a lake or river shore cleanup, planting trees, or even helping with recycling ventures. Any little bit helps.

49. Test Your Patience With Origami

For those who want to test their manual dexterity and creativity, origami is the fun act of creating beautiful shapes and figures using paper. You can find a book on the topic, connect with a local or online group, or watch online tutorials on YouTube to get an idea of how to start creating simple pieces and then move on to more complex ones.

This is another option for the cost-conscious retiree. A piece of paper and an abundance of patience is all that is required to make beautiful sculptures. There are an infinite number of patterns and options. This is also a great activity to create those special and unique holiday decorations.

Key Takeaways

Overall, remember that these hobbies and interests are a great way to build on existing activities in your life, or as a starting point for you. You don't have to try all of them; just the ones that do interest you or that you have some kind of connection with. This is the time to act on those "I've always wanted to try that" thoughts.

Having a hobby is a great way to enjoy life, as you get to do something that gives you a sense of satisfaction and fulfillment. Always try to have at least one hobby that keeps you occupied, entertained, challenged, or fulfilled, and happy during the quiet times in life.

Let's continue on to the next chapter of our book, which looks at options for making money as a side hustle or business.

Chapter 5:

Running a Business or Making Supplemental Income

For most of our lives, we work, so that we can earn money to support ourselves and our families. Retirement doesn't mean that you have to stop finding ways to earn money if you choose, because you still can!

In the previous chapters, we have looked at some ideas that you could use to have fun, stay fit, and maintain social connections. Now it's time to move on to our next group of fun ideas, which will help make money to supplement your retirement funds while possibly fulfilling a dream to start/progress your own business. This may not be because you need to earn the cash, but having a side hustle is another type of hobby or interest, especially if it's a byproduct of something that you like to do. For example, I have always enjoyed traveling, reading, and writing, so once I retired, I decided to author my own travel book. Quite an exhilarating side hustle I must say.

Part-Time Work or a Side Hustle?

There are more than a few ways to earn money while doing something you enjoy or something that you've always wanted to try but didn't have the time to prior to retiring. Many of us were encouraged to take a different career path initially, either because someone persuaded us that writing wasn't a job or making enough money singing to support a family was unrealistic, or we needed a steady paycheck from an established employer.

Now that you are retired, you can choose to go back to something that you've always wanted to do to give you another source of income. You can invest as much time, effort, and money in establishing your business and profile as you see fit.

Let's look at a variety of options that can help you make money while you stay engaged in the process of doing what you love.

50. Sell Your Art and Crafts

Most of us have some kind of talent. If you are a creative person and you have the tendency to make beautiful art pieces, crafting jewelry, handmade woodwork, or even steelwork, you can always choose to sell your crafts. You can establish an online presence or a website store and market your product online. Using the information provided in each of the previous chapters as reference, you can sell your product through a variety of methods.

If you choose to take up photography as one of your hobbies, you can post your pictures on one of the websites such as *Unsplash* or *Pexels*. People can select your photo for their use, and even give you a gratuity in the form of money or a coffee voucher.

51. Start a Business

People have many ideas for starting their own business. Some of us dream of marketing our own product as mentioned above, or can offer a service as a business. For example, someone I know used their love of reading and writing, along with their attention to detail, to start their own copyediting and proofreading business after retiring from a demanding corporate job. Combining their passions in a number of areas has afforded this person the opportunity to make money at their own pace, at home, doing something they enjoy and are good at. Ideal if you ask me!

If you are looking for something more established, you can become your own boss selling makeup and beauty products for companies like Avon. There are a lot of options for this kind of franchise business, so do some investigating online, through social groups, or your community.

52. Earn Through Passive Income

If you've always wanted to try out a business in the hospitality sector, you can try renting a spare room in your home or a property of yours on sites like VRBO or Airbnb. This is a great way for you to earn a passive income. All you need to do is advertise your home, put up some pictures on the website, set up competitive prices, and manage your bookings. Once advertised, you are not required to do much except make sure your property is maintained.

When you do get bookings, you will need to prepare the necessary space for all of your guests and ensure that you are giving them a pleasant experience. One of the most important aspects of running a property or room for rent is ensuring that the area is safe, clean, and comfortable for your guests. Providing a top-notch experience will lead to great reviews and more bookings.

53. Sell Produce From Your Garden

If one of your hobbies is gardening, and you have quite a bit of space for growing a variety of products in your garden, you may want to consider selling some of whatever you grow. This is a great way to earn income from one of your hobbies because you are investing the time and effort into your garden regardless of what you produce. It depends on how much you want to grow and how much you want to sell.

You may need a permit to sell produce, which should be obtained if you are considering this option. Also, whatever you don't sell or need, look into donating to a local food bank or charity. Any opportunity to help the food deprived and cut down on waste is a valuable option

54. Do Odd Jobs While you Travel

Another fun way to earn an income from a side hustle or a part-time job is to perform odd jobs at a campground if you are traveling. There could be opportunities such as office work, maintenance, cleaning, hospitality, and similar responsibilities available. You can talk to the campground operator to see if you can do any odd jobs in exchange for your stay. Who knows, you might be able to take your RV across the country and not have to pay for any campground stays this way.

55. House or Pet Sit

This is a great way to earn some extra cash without doing much work. When it comes to house or pet sitting, there are websites where you can connect with people who need these services. The benefit of having these websites is that the fee you charge and the payment is all controlled by the platform, so you know that this is a trustworthy site with legitimate customers too. In some cases, the pay will be minimal, but having an accommodation in a location you have considered visiting may be the ideal trade off.

Combining house sitting with travel can provide the best of both worlds and give you cost effective opportunities to see the world. You can even offer reciprocal housing options. With pet sitting, be sure you are comfortable and take the opportunity to meet the animal prior to committing to their care.

56. Become a Handy Person

You can use your skills and fix-it know-how to help others who may need someone to complete some odd jobs at their house. First, make sure that you evaluate your skills and interests to know exactly what you can do in areas such as plumbing, electrical work, home maintenance, and even carpentry. You can advertise yourself as a retired professional if you are still licensed or maintaining credentials in a specific skill area. Be clear on what type of work you cannot take on as well.

Other seniors in your community will welcome your help. You can build a reputation through word of mouth, and advertise through your local seniors center or community center.

57. Be a Freelance Writer or Ghost Writer

Another great way to earn money is by becoming a freelance writer. If you've had a passion for writing books or articles that range from entertainment, sports, and hobbies to health and wellness, then this is a great way for you to turn your passion into a profit. You can advertise your services on your social media platforms, such as Facebook, Instagram, or similar media, stating that you are an aspiring writer. If you have some experience writing, you can attach samples to your portfolio, or offer a minimal word sample of a potential client's work for free.

There are many sites available online where you can register and bid on work items. Look for sites that hire writers such as TUW, Upwork, or Fiverr and submit your application to them. Once you create a profile, you can begin accepting orders. You can become more selective with your workload once you have built a following.

58. Review Books for Cash

If writing isn't your thing but reading is, you can find work as a book reviewer online. There are many sites geared to finding readers for this job. Budding authors and publishers often seek people to read their publications and provide honest reviews.

While most writers will look for free reviews, you can find options for paid reviews. Some platforms, like Amazon, discourage paid reviews, thinking that someone being paid for a review may be less likely to post an honest review. Companies like *Reedsy* or *WordsRated* do offer payment for book reviews.

59. Teach a Course

Are you good at teaching people? Do you love sharing knowledge with others, especially younger adults, or children? Or maybe you have pictured yourself at the front of a lecture hall facing students thirsting for the knowledge you can share. Then teaching part time is one great way to earn some extra cash while pursuing a subject of your interest. There are so many topics at schools or colleges, depending on your qualifications. Be it science, history, geography, the environment, math, or English you can choose your own topic according to your past experience and go for it. If your time is flexible, see if you can get your name on the substitute teachers list in your area.

Attending online courses became the norm for many during the pandemic, and this option continues to be viable for many learners. Create a virtual course in your

area of interest, or even record a live session and distribute online.

60. Drive for a Ride-Share Service

Services like Uber or Bolt are always looking for drivers. If you have a car, love to drive, can navigate a map, and follow Siri's directions, this might just be the side hustle for you. You never know who will be looking for a ride or where the next fare will go. This is a great way to earn a part-time income at your leisure. Be sure to check with your insurance company though before proceeding.

Driving for a ride-share or even a delivery service like DoorDash or UberEats can be a great way to make some extra cash. You can schedule your own availability through these vendors, and work as much or as little as you choose.

Key Takeaways

The content in this chapter introduced you to some of the most popular ideas for earning a side income from part-time work and sales. They don't require too much effort from you and you can invest as much time and effort as you like. You get to do the things that you've always wanted to do, meet people in the process, and obtain a new income stream. This is a great way to achieve a number of your goals in one activity.

Supplementing your pension and retirement income is more common as the cost of living increases. Many of us who planned for retirement based on a specific income have found that we need to supplement that amount or adjust it to make the most of our retirement dollars. Do make sure you research the tax implications of any additional income you make over and above your pension.

Some of the suggestions made here may have triggered thoughts of formal education. Let's move on to the next chapter which revolves around continued education, learning new skills, and even completing that elusive degree. It's all about the fun of learning!

Chapter 6:

Embracing Education— Fun Ways to Challenge Your Mind

Age is just a number and the thought of how old you are should not stop you from learning or pursuing higher education. We learn something new every day, even from our mistakes. Formal education helps us expand our knowledge base through structured programs. We need to keep our minds stimulated and active as much as possible in our later years. If we do not keep up with the fast paced world we will find it difficult to involve cognitive thinking and use our memory as time moves on.

There are many enjoyable opportunities to educate yourself and learn. This chapter will look at a few of the fun and inspiring education options available to you in your retirement.

Discover Something New

There is no end to learning and this can involve fun and activities at the same time. You can learn new things and discover something that you had no idea about. I will discuss them here to let you choose and discover something interesting yourself.

61. Learn a New Skill

Take the opportunity in your retirement to learn a new skill. Know that you are not limited to just one idea. You can try out as many as you like. There are a variety of skills that you could learn depending on your interests, and each one is different in its level of creativity and intellect. Some of the skills that you could try include a few we mentioned in the hobbies and interests chapter, such as painting, photography, learning how to play a musical instrument, carpentry, restoration, and geocaching.

The new skill you pursue may be more along the academic lines, such as technical, writing, or data analysis. This can purely be for interest or as a base for a new business venture. For example, enhancing your financial knowledge and bookkeeping skills can help with budgeting.

62. Complete a Degree

It may sound a little daunting, but why not go back to school? You could enroll in college or university and attend as a senior. You may wish to pursue a certain degree or even just attend for personal enrichment. You can go to school for a variety of reasons, all of which are built on the foundation of learning a new skill, acquiring a new certification, or the chance to complete a dream.

I know many retirees that jump at the chance to complete a long desired bucket list item to gain their diploma, bachelors, masters, or PhD, now that they have the time to pursue this option that may have eluded them when earning money to support the home took priority. It can be quite rewarding to gain that designation that may have been out of reach during your work life.

63. Learn a New Language or Two

Learning a new language is something you will find interesting as well as educational. The main benefit of learning a new language is that it helps improve your memory and enhances your problem-solving skills. It also improves your cognitive skills. When you know and can speak more than one language you'll find it especially useful when you travel. Being able to communicate with others in their language can open doors for you culturally.

It doesn't have to be one language; you can learn two or more languages and increase your linguistic skills. Applications like Babble enable you to learn a language from anywhere, like while you are driving or cooking dinner. The conversational nature of the language means you are learning phrases you will be able to use immediately and regularly.

64. Take Classes That Interest You

When it comes to classes, they don't always have to be in college or at a university. There are so many other types of continuing education or interest classes that offer information as well as teach you how to do a certain task and develop skills around various subjects. Similar to activity number 61. *Learn a New Skill* included at the start of this chapter, you can take a course or class on any number of interests. In this case, the focus is on an interest you may have, like medieval history, or Thai cooking. This is a great way for you to learn something new through a structured program that may be hosted online or even in person at your local community or senior center. It is also a great way to keep your mind active and your curiosity burning. You can take a variety of classes at the same time or finish one at a time.

One of the most commonly used sources of learning today is online learning. The main benefits include not having to travel to a specific place and having access to the class. Learning through online sources is flexible and can assist you in more ways than one. You are learning at your own speed, at a pace that is comfortable for you.

65. Join a Book Club

If you love to read, know that your mind will be kept engaged while you learn new things from the books and articles that you read. If you love books and enjoy discussing the content, then a great activity for you to try out would be to join a book club or a reading group. Most book clubs meet once a month to discuss the assigned literary piece. The genres can vary each month, providing the opportunity to delve into an area you might otherwise avoid.

By joining a book club, you may get to meet new people and make new connections while having stimulating discussions on topics you find interesting from these books. You can expand your literary horizons by coming into contact with people who have the same passion for reading as you do.

66. Attend Workshops and Conferences

If you are looking for another way to learn new things you can attend workshops, seminars or conferences pertaining to your interests. For example, as an author, I love to expand my knowledge by attending publishing conferences. I can combine my love of travel, enhance my brand visibility, and learn more about being an author by attending a conference full of like-minded individuals. And, if you do have your own registered business (see activity 51. *Start a Business* for ideas) you can claim most if not all your expenses through your company.

If you have decided to focus on greenhouse gardening in your retirement, there are workshops to help you design and build the structure as well as what to grow, how to irrigate your plants, and how to control pests. Regardless of your interest, there are support avenues out there for you.

67. Engage in Brain Training Activities

The next fun idea for keeping your brain active and engaged is to try out some brain training activities. Such activities keep your mind sharp and your memory skills strong. Items that focus on brain activity include complex word puzzles, number puzzles like Sudoku, escape rooms, and those involving trivia, such as Jeopardy. Wordle has become one of the most popular ones in recent years. You can combine game night with a trip to your local pub for themed quiz events.

There are many brain-training apps that you can find online. If you have a smartphone, go to your app store, and search for brain-training apps. If not, you can use your laptop computer to find out which game you can play that challenges your thinking and problem-solving skills or even a game that is designed specifically to boost your memory.

68. Volunteer in Educational Settings

Something many people don't think about is the enhanced learning benefit they themselves can gain from volunteering in educational settings. This can be in school or public libraries, or even adult education centers. Volunteering in educational settings can be a rewarding experience for all involved. You get to observe firsthand how others learn and what education methods work for different groups. You can enrich your life while offering your time to a worthwhile venture.

Literacy is an area often seeking volunteers. Helping people enhance their English skills and reading levels can lead someone to employment or job advancement. There are organizations that promote literacy skills. Contacting them may open doors for you to help someone become more confident with their reading and writing.

69. Explore Online Webinars, Podcasts, and TED Talks

Another great way for you to learn new things and keep your mind engaged is by watching webinars, or listening to podcasts, and TED talks. The latter—standing for Technology, Entertainment, Design—are a more recent learning option. TED is a non-profit organization that hosts education sessions on topics under these three broad categories, and provides the recordings for public view online. They are short, approximately 18-20 minutes long recordings.

If you want to know more about these education options, visit websites that offer free educational videos, such as TED.com, or you could visit specialized education websites such as GoToWebinar or Zoom Webinars that give you access to these TED talks and webinars.

70. Enhance Your Technical Knowledge

A high percentage of what we do every day involves technology. We can only use the information we are able to locate online. If we can't find information because we aren't comfortable with the tools we use, research will be lacking. There is truth to the statement that today's children are more advanced technically than many seniors.

In Chapter 3, the first activity listed is 26. *Plan Your Trip*, which involves extensive research. While it is true there are many avenues to follow to find information without using the internet, the most current information and reviews are found online. Being comfortable with your technology and adept at finding accurate information quickly will help you tremendously with the majority of your activities.

Key Takeaways

Educating yourself with so many options available to expand your knowledge will help you retire. Choose any one of the ways mentioned above and you can spend a quality time either learning or teaching others. Make this opportunity a successful journey and share your own knowledge to the world. You never know when or how you could make a huge difference and make the most of your free time in retirement. Completing that dream degree or spending time with the latest online education options such as TED talks are ideal and easily accessible from your home computer. We also looked at some classroom, workshop, and conference ideas to build on opportunities introduced in earlier chapters.

Moving on, it is time now to look inward and consider options for enhancing your spirituality in retirement.

Chapter 7:

Nurturing Your Spiritual Self and Personal Development

Human beings are more than just their bodies and minds. We have a spiritual aspect to us. This is what we refer to as our souls. Spirituality is also called "divinity" by some cultures such as Buddhists, Christians, Hinduism, and Native Americans. It is the state in which you reach a higher level, bringing yourself closer to God, the universe, a worshiped supreme being, or in other words your "higher self." This does not have to be through any formal type of worship either, the deep belief is the most important aspect.

You must bring all aspects of your body, mind, physical health, and your spiritual health into perfect order to feel whole. This will give you an overall sense of well-being as well as fulfillment.

By learning more about your inner self, you get to explore your spirituality and nurture your personal growth as you find a sense of purpose and deeper meaning in your life. There are many practices of meditation, prayer, or mindfulness, to name a few, to accomplish this.

How to Nurture Your Spirituality and Enhance Personal Development

Basically, personal growth and self-reflection through spirituality will help you become self-aware and improve your spiritual self. Know that these ideas are fun exercises that also come with a variety of benefits.

71. Cultivate Gratitude and Positive Thinking

When it comes to personal development and spiritual growth, the first thing that you would need to change within is your manner of thinking. You must have gratitude as well as a positive mindset to personally grow and achieve happiness. One way to achieve this is by keeping a gratitude journal in which you can write down ways to show your gratitude. Expressing gratitude to others will feed your positivity. Listing and repeating positive statements and affirmations throughout the day and/or putting up sticky notes everywhere to reinforce the habit helps to maintain a positive attitude. And smile! A lot.

The most important benefit that you receive from having a positive mindset and a grateful attitude is your perspective on life. When you are constantly positive, you approach life with a "can do" attitude. A positive mindset will promote a healthier outlook and overall well-being, and will help you navigate challenges more effectively.

72. Explore Your Spiritual Self

Exploring your spiritual self is a personal journey where you reflect inward and learn to visualize your life with a positive perspective. You are connecting with something beyond and greater than yourself. This is where you reflect on your beliefs and values, as well as what brings meaning to your life. Write your thoughts out in a journal and reflect on them. You consider what you went through in the past as well as what has resonated with you on a spiritual level. Determine what you feel drawn toward.

This is not necessarily a religious journey. Many people feel a deep sense of spirituality without being devoted to a specific religion. Your spirituality is what you make it, and the way you choose to express your faith.

73. Try Meditation Training

Incorporating meditation into your daily routine provides an infinite number of benefits. This will help you cultivate mindfulness, which means that you are fully present and in the moment. You can observe your thoughts and whatever emotions you feel without any judgment. This helps you quiet your mind as well as develop inner peace and self-discovery. Start small and then increase your duration as you become more comfortable meditating.

Meditation is closely tied to one of the first activities introduced in this book, 3. *Become Flexible With Yoga*. Practicing a combination of these two activities can provide the centering and grounding you need for self-reflection.

74. Engage in Mindfulness Practices

Mindfulness is the practice of maintaining a nonjudgmental state of heightened or complete awareness of one's thoughts, emotions, or experiences on a moment-to-moment basis (Webster, 2023). It is the state of committing your thoughts fully on whatever activity you are currently completing. Mindfulness practices are a great way for you to discover who you are on a personal level as well as develop your spiritual self. This includes activities such as mindfulness training, mindfulness meditation, deep breathing exercises, and even mindful eating.

Mindfulness and meditation often go hand-in-hand. This increased awareness channels your focus to the here and now. The idea is to be present in the moment, blocking extraneous thoughts from your mind, and bringing your focus to what you can see, do, smell, and feel in the present moment.

75. Join a Bible Study Group

The benefits of joining a bible study group through your church or community is the opportunity to discuss the implications of the scripture on the present with people who are also curious about their faith and its roots. A group can help you engage in spiritual activities that bring positivity. Religious groups composed of like-minded people may help you question and reflect on your beliefs more. You will find the support and motivation you need for your journey.

76. Take Religious Classes or Workshops

There are opportunities for you to take religious classes or workshops. When you enroll in them, you get exposed to more opportunities to find new information about religion and its role in human life. These classes can be fun and exciting as you get to learn with other like-minded people and talk about religion and participate in the workshops in groups. Consider taking a course or workshop in faiths outside of your own.

77. Participate in Personal Development Courses

Personal development is a way to enhance your skills, be it spiritual, cognitive, physical, or one specific area you want to improve. Personal development courses can help guide you on your journey for personal fulfillment. There are a variety of topics that you can choose from, which include creative writing classes, art classes, life coaching programs, anger management, and more. You can use the basic method of obtaining these courses online, or you could even visit your local university or college and find out whether they offer such personal development courses. Senior centers are also a great resource for retiree focused personal development. When it comes to personal development courses, make sure that you choose those that align with your interests and goals.

When you delve into personal discovery, you will notice that you are growing in not just understanding who you are but also in living to your full potential. You are working towards developing and even honing your skills so that you become the type of individual you have always been, but better!

78. Attend a Wellness Retreat

Picture yourself communing with nature and the environment, far away from all of life's daily demands. A wellness retreat may just be the thing to center yourself. These retreats can take many forms, but all focus on you and your overall health and well-being. Pampering the soul seems like an appropriate activity in your retirement, doesn't it?

There are a variety of benefits that can be obtained from these mind-body-spirit practices introduced at these retreats, which involve practicing gentle movements, and stretching as well as deep breathing techniques. These activities enhance your physical health, fitness, flexibility, and balance.

79. Learn About Blue Zones: Lessons in Longevity

Did you already know about something called "blue zones?" These are specific regions in the world where people live longer and much healthier lives compared to the global average population. When studying these areas, it was found that common lifestyle and cultural factors were the reasons that contributed to the longevity of these inhabitants. Most of these people changed to eating a plant-based diet with little or moderate calorie intake. They exercise regularly and socialize to reduce stress and have a purposeful life.

By incorporating all of the activities and the lessons learned from each one, such as plant-based eating, socializing with others using various methods to keep happy and occupied, and finding a deeper meaning in your life through personal development and spiritual journeys, you can live an incredible life that is healthy and long. Basically, you get enhanced well-being.

80. Create a Gratitude Calendar

One way to reinforce your personal development is to create a calendar of affirmations. Each day, add something new to your journey toward positivity, gratitude, self-reflection, and well-being. It could be a one-word sticky note, reminding yourself to smile. Another day might be a bible reference, or a reflection on a kindness you received from someone. Think of all the enrichment you will have in your life after 365 days!

List a number of points on the things that make you feel grateful about in life. There are so many topics and thoughts on creating a calendar. It might even help you explore your own life achievements and bring back some good memories from the past. When you learn to show gratitude you can improve your relationships and well-being. Your mental health is improved a lot through the process. These are some notes you can add to your calendar and fill in each box everyday with new things to do with a table like this:

Share Love	Show Gratitude	Good Things Happened This Week	Appreciate Something You Own	Pay It Forward

Key Takeaways

Know that if you aren't a religious person, you aren't forced to visit a religious organization or attend any of their services. You can choose whichever direction you feel most comfortable with. Meet someone who practices meditation and yoga regularly. They can provide tips on ways to practice introspection.

There are a variety of local institutions as well as online platforms that offer religious education programs. However, if you are not too keen on visiting any of the local institutions, you can go to the local services and find out from a religious leader where exactly you can go for religious classes.

Next, let's look at ways you can use your new or renewed sense of self to help others through charitable efforts and volunteering.

Chapter 8:

Giving Back Through

Charity and Volunteering

Retirement provides the opportunity for you to be more charitable with your time. Being a volunteer in any capacity has benefits for both the giver and recipient. During our working years, while we may have been able to help out in person on occasion, our charitable contributions were more likely financial than time-based.

In this chapter, the focus is on how we can give back, who receives our generous gifts, and where we can find charitable, volunteer opportunities.

Fun, Charitable Ideas

Combining fun activities with giving back to charities is a win-win for everyone involved. Let's look at some of these options.

81. Mentor Others

Mentoring is a meaningful way to share your knowledge and pass along your skills, as well as your life experiences. Your audience can be younger, older, or a group of your peers—anyone who can benefit from the experience you offer. For example, if you were a certified project manager during your career, you could volunteer to mentor other PMs through the examination process. This is a way for you to make a positive impact in other people's lives by providing beneficial information and utilizing all the skills you built during your career.

If you are interested in becoming a mentor for a specific group or on a specific topic, investigate the most appropriate avenue for you to follow. You might want to reach out to other retirees from your former employer or in your social circle to learn what route they would suggest you follow.

If you want to be a good mentor you need to be a good listener, trustworthy, honest, and candid. A good mentor will have a good camaraderie with a colleague or friend he or she is sharing knowledge with. Note that there is no age limit for being a mentor.

82. Feed the Hungry and Homeless

Two ongoing issues that many communities face with their constituents are hunger and homelessness. Many people are still struggling in the post-pandemic economy. There are so many families and communities where people are suffering and cannot make ends meet. Those families may turn to food banks and shelters for support.

By getting involved, either by finding funding to support the homeless and food-deprived in your community or by volunteering at a soup kitchen (for example) you are providing a much needed set of hands to a worthwhile cause. Non-profit and charitable organizations that provide these services are always looking for dependable people to help.

83. Donate Produce From Your Garden

This is an opportunity to build on one of the previous activities we discussed in Chapter 2; activity number 20. *Join or Create a Community Garden.* We mentioned selling some of the produce as a side hustle activity (53. *Sell Produce From Your Garden*) but donating some can be rewarding and provide those in need with the fresh vegetables they may otherwise not get. You could even have a section of the community garden dedicated specifically to growing produce for donation. You could even have some of those receiving the food come to help harvest it, providing them with stake in its success.

By coming up with a community garden, you will be able to help many people, not only in your local community but in nearby neighborhoods as well. This is a great way for you to collaborate with your local community members to come together and succeed, feeding at least one person at a time.

84. Organize a Fundraiser

If you have the knowledge and can organize a fundraising venture, this can be one of the most effective ways to help charitable organizations. Charities, by nature, are giving entities, and having the help of people who can organize giving opportunities is an asset. Some of the most popular fundraising activities include bottle drives, dances, and silent auctions.

Here are some steps you can follow to raise funds:

- Establish your goal for raising funds.

- Inform donors, philanthropists, and supporters of your objective.

- Circulate information in the area or neighborhood you want to impact.

- Establish a fixed budget for your cause.

- Gather a proficient team who will share your passion for this fundraising event.

- Schedule a date for your event well in advance, in order for participants to book their attendance.

- Market your event through all possible means, such as direct mail, email, text messages, word of mouth, or social media

- Communicate the status of your fundraiser with your clients, members, and donors.

- Make your fundraising fun and enjoyable.

85. Foster Rescue Animals

If you are an animal lover, part of your retirement can be spent helping animal welfare organizations. I know the shelters have been hit hard since the pandemic, with people finding they can no longer care for pets, whether young or old. Many people acquired their pet during the pandemic, when being homebound afforded the opportunity to devote the time and energy to the animal's care. In turn, the pet provided the companionship people needed.

Post-pandemic however, with the significant downturn of the economy, people struggle to care for themselves and put food on the table, let alone provide the same for their pet as well. The rate of animals being abandoned and requiring new homes has risen and the need for foster homes has increased dramatically.

86. Serve on a Non-Profit Board

Put your leadership skills to work as a board member for a local non-profit, not-for-profit, or charitable organization. Helping to provide the necessary oversight for these organizations is a valuable and rewarding activity. You may already be affiliated with an organization, or now have the time as a retiree to pursue this avenue.

This is a great way to help provide guidance to an organization. If you have limited visibility to the group, you may be even more valuable helping to promote the product or philosophy of the organization.

87. Help With Disaster Relief Efforts

The environment is volatile with the impact of climate change. Every day, there are reports of severe, violent storms, hurricanes, and tornados. If you have ever had a leak in your basement, you know on a smaller scale the damage water can do. Imagine the tragedy of the water washing away your home, your neighbors houses, and the community around you. The impact is devastating and any available time, skills, and resources you can contribute to the cleanup efforts would be most welcome. Need to know more? Contact your local support groups to see where your efforts are best suited.

Check the sites for programs that are located near your neighborhood such as renowned organizations (USAID, UNFPA, WHO) that take care of disasters all around the globe. While you research a bit on these organizations you will know more about situations prevailing in many countries around the world. You don't have to travel far to help the refugees or people who are struck with natural disasters around the globe.

Another active organization that provides disaster relief and post-emergency services is the Red Cross. This organization works with disaster stricken countries everywhere outside and within the United States. You can visit their website to find out more about their supporting role in financial assistance and providing grants at the community level.

88. Volunteer at a Hospital or Nursing Home

You may remember the days when hospital volunteers were called candy stripers. Young women, predominantly high school or college age wore a red (or pink) and white striped pinafore while volunteering their help (Candy Stripers: A Journey of Hospital Volunteers in the United States, 2023).

No, you don't have to wear that uniform if you volunteer these days. Your time is valuable to perform a number of functions to make a hospital stay a bit brighter for a patient, or give the nursing staff a moment to breathe. Nursing homes welcome an extra set of hands to assist in the nursing or elder care homes. The volunteer pool diminished significantly during and since the Covid pandemic, so an hour you can give is valuable and welcomed.

There are hospitals and healthcare places such as the Atlantic Health System where seniors can volunteer at their medical centers and share skills or spend quality time with other senior patients (*Volunteer Opportunities-Senior Services*, 2023).

89. Take Your Professional Skill Overseas

If you are a retired medical professional, or are skilled in carpentry (for example), consider using your skills to help those in a less advanced nation. For example, *Doctors Without Borders* is a well-known organization where medical professionals contribute their time and skills to the needy in other countries. This is a chance to make use of your skills as well as gain importance or recognition internationally.

Skilled labor of almost any nature is valuable to those in less affluent countries and locations. If you love to travel, you can combine tourist activities with giving back to local communities. This could bring back some lovely memories of the past when you had to travel for work or important site visits. Travelling has been covered before and I am sure you understand there is no one who can give up this great opportunity.

90. Read to Elementary School Children

Most teachers will welcome the help in their classrooms. One of the best ways to provide help is to read either to the class as a whole, or with small groups of students. There may be rules about grade levels and supervision, and a police background check may be required, but if the school board allows it, this is a rewarding social activity.

Reading to children can be relaxing and fun at the same time. Choose a familiar topic, like animals, unless the school provides one and talk about the book to explain what the story is about. You can also add some of your own insights and experience into the discussion which may be more interesting to the class and might even intrigue them to ask questions.

Key Takeaways

To summarize, there are more than just a few ideas that you could try out to change even one person's life. Promoting literacy is giving someone self-confidence while they learn a life skill. Your contribution doesn't have to be financial, though many charities prefer money in order to channel it to the resources required.

Contributing a small generous act or changing one person's life at a time is more than enough. Volunteering and giving your time or money is extremely rewarding. As long as you are happy giving, then you are already a success at charity work and volunteering.

Let's turn our focus to sustenance now, real food for the soul.

Chapter 9:

Food for the Soul: Healthy Eating, Cooking, and Takeout

Our next group of fun ideas include nourishing your body and soul with healthy cooking, eating, and takeout. The latter may or may not be healthy, but there are so many delicious offerings. It is particularly important that, as you age, you maintain a healthy lifestyle, and this includes the kind of foods that you eat.

We'll look at some fun culinary ideas for trying out different types of foods and cuisines that offer a variety of benefits to your body. This is a great way for you to learn about different cultures and the types of foods that they enjoy eating. At the same time, you are keeping your own body fit and healthy in the process. Let's go over a few ideas that you could try out to have fun while keeping your body healthy with the right types of food.

Before changing your diet significantly, you should speak to your healthcare provider. Making any sudden changes in nourishment, while usually positive, may affect medication you are taking. Or you might require supplemental vitamins or nutrients. Some people cannot go on a diet that excludes food products from animals, as they may need proteins and vitamin B supplements that can boost their bodies and help with various ailments.

Fun Food Ideas

91. Try Different Cultural Restaurants

I found the Mongolian Grill and am hooked. It can be hard to try new foods, let alone at a restaurant where you may be immersed in a foreign culture. If you haven't had the opportunity prior to retiring, consider trying at least one new cultural food experience each month. Make reservations at a Japanese teppanyaki room one month and a Mediterranean themed restaurant the next. The options are endless and you may just find a new favorite!

Depending on where you live, you may or may not have access to a variety of restaurants. The larger the city, and the more culturally diverse its inhabitants, the more opportunities exist.

Tasting different cultural foods can help you discover the similarities or differences between other countries and yours. For instance, there are some common staples like bread, butter, or pasta consumed in many parts of South Korea which are familiar to those of the US or European countries. Potatoes, tomatoes, pepper and many more ingredients are common all over the world. In Asian countries rice and hand-made wheat breads or flat breads are common. You can mix and match some of these items to your meals as well.

92. Attempt Climate-Friendly and Sustainable Eating

Something new that has been introduced recently is climate-friendly and sustainable eating. This is basically where you eat the types of foods that are beneficial to not only yourself but the environment as well. Some beneficial information on sustainable food practices includes reducing the amount of meat that you consume. It involves you being encouraged to choose local and organic products instead of imported and processed foods. Another great way to be environmentally conscious is to minimize the amount of food wasted.

By eating environmentally friendly foods, you are keeping the planet clean, green, and in much better shape than when you constantly have a diet that isn't climate-friendly. Another great benefit is the fact that these foods are more organic and locally sourced, so they are much healthier for your overall well-being. Local support helps the economy and eliminates transportation.

Here are some tips on how to follow sustainable eating:

- Meat production contributes to a large amount of greenhouse gas emitted: Eat less meat to lower the demand on livestock which will in turn lower the stress on natural resources.

- Choose an alternative resource: If you can switch your diet towards seafood items more it can help you improve your health with constituents like omega-3, vitamins, and other minerals.

- Explore local markets: If you can get an opportunity to visit your local markets and learn about how food was produced and harvested then it can help you understand more about their sources.

- Eat mindfully: This practice is one of the best ways to follow a safe and healthy diet. It also helps you to maintain a balance in your food consumption without having to deal with wastes.

93. Test Vegan or Plant-Based Nutrition

You can explore different types of diets that suit you. There is a difference between vegan and plant-based diets. The former option excludes animal-derived products, so even honey, eggs, milk, and other products aren't eaten. However, when you have a plant-based diet, this doesn't mean that you exclude animal-derived products. You can eat honey and milk, but the main focus is on plant-based foods like whole grains, nuts, seeds, vegetables, and more.

There are more than a few benefits that come from having a plant-based diet or going vegan. You will become much healthier, as all plant-based foods are protected foods and give your body the essential vitamins and minerals it needs to stay healthy. Also, your digestive system will be functioning well, as most plant-based foods contain fiber. You can also receive other benefits such as improved memory, a better ability to fight off illness and disease, and an overall sense of well-being.

94. Test Online Nutrition Counseling

You could try online nutrition counseling. There are numerous food and nutrition oriented counseling services offered to help with either meal planning or to address dietary concerns. There are even sites that are specifically tailored to assist with a senior's dietary needs and goals.

Nutrition counseling is getting personal guidance of your diet and food intake. This helps you to follow a healthier life that is free from illness. At a certain age we need to follow a good diet and healthy lifestyle. This can be done through counseling or talking to someone professional.

Dieticians and nutritional counselors are specifically trained to look at a holistic view of a client's needs. Looking at the big picture allows for menu planning that can accommodate lifestyle, food likes and dislikes, as well as any sensitivities like gluten, lactose, or tree nuts.

These are the steps followed in nutrition counseling sessions:

- Reviewing your general health and medical history.

- Understanding the basic nutrition needs.

- Teaching you how to make mindful choices for your diet.

- Setting a goal for your nutrition plan.

- Personalizing your nutrition plan.

A nutrition plan can vary significantly from one person to another which is why you need a good one to one counseling.

95. Try Community Cooking Classes

As discussed in some of the earlier chapters, your local seniors community center is a valuable source of information and programs for retirees. If your center offers cooking classes, this is an opportunity for you to socialize, prepare a meal, and learn a new skill if you are not already proficient in the kitchen.

Another option is to get together with a group and prepare meals using old family recipes. Each person in the group could make a family recipe, and even share with the group the memories that particular dish has for them.

An advantage of community cooking classes is to cook themed dishes for special days such as Christmas, Thanksgiving, the 4th of July, or any national holiday. Enjoy the holidays with your cooking class and it could turn into a party for you all. You can also enhance your cooking space or room with beautiful colored ribbons, lights, and festive decorations .

96. Investigate Cooking-for-One Options

If you are single, you may find planning meals, selecting ingredients, and preparing the food too much of a bother. The ingredients alone can be expensive, especially if you need to buy all the spices in regular quantities. You may never use them again, or they'll expire before you do. Investing in a good single serving cookbook or researching options online can help you with suggestions for food shopping as well as multiple recipes for using specific ingredients. An alternative to prepackaged items, consider shopping in the bulk foods section where you can purchase only the amounts you need.

Probiotics are a good option to include in your diet. Science suggests that probiotics are the good bacteria that are present in certain fermented foods, and they help keep your body, digestive system, and overall well-being healthy. They do more than just help with digestion; they also help to produce and maintain certain hormones. Probiotics can be found in foods such as kefir, sauerkraut, and kimchi.

Research some fermented foods and get your daily dose of probiotics from them. Do remember that you cannot introduce a whole lot of fermented foods into your diet if you haven't eaten them before. Like everything else, start slowly and then increase the amount ever so slowly. This is basically so that you can avoid an upset stomach.

97. Test Different Takeout Options

During the pandemic, if a restaurant wanted to remain viable, it had to provide a non-contact takeout and/or delivery option. Many establishments continue offering these services, which provide a wealth of options beyond the traditional Chinese food and pizza. There is nothing wrong with those options, believe me, but being able to try out different foods at home is fantastic.

The introduction of food delivery services like UberEats, Skip the Dishes and DoorDash help make the options more accessible as well. People are more receptive to trying different options when they are accessible.

98. Host or Attend a Potluck

I love pot luck lunches and dinners (hhhhmmm, I don't think I have ever attended a potluck breakfast). This is a great opportunity to combine socializing with food, a perfect combination. No two are alike, and it is an opportunity to try foods you may not otherwise. You may have a couple of go-to dishes you usually take, so if you get the chance, take the opportunity to try something new.

There are so many ideas you can use for potluck parties. They could be color themed, where everyone has to bring a dish containing a certain color ingredient. Or, they could be culturally themed, or particular ingredients used such as chili, garlic, or rosemary. You could have so much fun planning your potluck. Here are some ideas you can try on your next event:

- Texas salsa

- Granola mix

- Cobb salad sub

- Hummus

- Garlic bean spread

- Pastrami roll ups

There are many more items you can find on Facebook groups or on food-related websites.

99. Take a Wine or Beer Tour

While not necessarily at the top of any nutritionist's list, participating in a wine or beer tour can expand your horizons. No drinking and driving involved, transportation is provided with these tours. Along with wine, you can learn about which cheeses pair well with each vintage.

If craft beer is more your style, there are definitely options that focus on this. While craft beer is a favorite of millennials (Blonnenberg et al., 2021), the options are available to all beer lovers.

100. Eat Crickets

Yes, you read that correctly, and no, I am not setting you up for an episode of Fear Factor! While many of us cringe at the thought, other cultures see this as a delicacy, or even a dietary staple. If you get the opportunity to wander through the street markets in some countries, you will be amazed at what you can find. Tarantulas are the choice in Cambodia, while the more common grasshoppers are in Mexico (Mccarthy, 2021).

Overcoming your fears is a part of this activity apart from tasting a new delicacy you just discovered. There are several markets in the south-east of Asia that sell these like candies and believe me, they do not look or taste the way you expected.

Key Takeaways

Throughout this chapter, we have focused on nutrition and most things foody related. As our daily lives change with retirement, so do our eating patterns and habits. It is easy to resort to the same old foods and recipes, and lose our adventurous spirit when it comes to nutrition. Trying new social options for dining, such as a new cultural restaurant or taking cooking classes broadens our options when it comes to what to have for dinner tonight. And throwing in a couple of juicy insects may not be as farfetched as you think!

In this chapter, we reached activity number 100, and we still have a wealth of adventures to investigate. Let's carry on, shall we?

Chapter 10:

Take It to the Extreme

This chapter will give fun and adventure a whole new meaning. Most of the activity options we have discussed in the previous chapters have been relatively safe. You haven't had to read the fine print in your insurance policy yet. It's time to shake things up, and look at some of the more extreme activities to test your will (creating/updating your will is activity 111 in the next chapter) and your adventurous spirit.

While it's great to seek fun, challenging, and exciting activities, safety comes first. Each of the activities we will discuss here have an element of danger, but can be completed with a modicum of safety. Be sure to research the activity operator where possible and read reviews from previous participants.

101. Go Skydiving

I have heard so many people say they have "always wanted to skydive, but…" Well, maybe now is the time. There are many companies that will take you up for a tandem dive, where you are literally and figuratively attached to an instructor for the duration of your jump.

You may want to go to an indoor skydiving facility first to test out the process.

A great example for skydiving where age is no barrier is Anna Mae Milnar. She fought cancer and at the age of 81 went skydiving for adventure. It proves how mentally strong and adventurous she is.

The Wisconsin Skydiving Center has even older participants at their venue adding this skill onto their bucket list.

To be able to skydive you may have to check a few points before going forward:

- Your heart has to be in good shape

- You need to be mobile and to be able to land with your legs

- Your general health should be good

- You must have some adventurous blood in you (*Skydiving Age Limit: Can You Be Too Old ?*, 2016).

Even if you are not sure of the answers to the above points, you can still go and have a session with the instructors. If you have any questions they can always help you.

102. Try Bungee Jumping Over a Gorge

Most of the larger amusement parks have added a bungee jump or slingshot type of activity to their offerings. These are certainly an adoption to tick the activity off your list, but for a real thrill, plan to complete this activity suspended over a raging gorge. That will get your blood pumping. Just don't look down. Until you have jumped, then take in a view of the landscape you will never get in any other form.

Somewhat similar to skydiving you must consider the points mentioned previously before going for bungee jumping. Any skill that requires free mobility and climbing or jumping from higher altitudes needs some guidance and a lot of courage.

Bungee jumping is considered dangerous to many when they hear of it but there are safe ways to complete this activity. To avoid injuries or discomfort you can go through a course of preparation with the professionals. These are the safety rules you can follow if you a real extreme sports person:

- Choose the perfect weather for your safety and avoid snow, wind, or extreme heat.

- Wear proper clothing such as fitted jackets and pants to avoid any loose clothing catching on anything. Also avoid using spectacles, jewelry, or contact lenses during extreme sports.

- Take as much training and preparation as you can, for example, test runs, rescue simulations, or maintenance of bungee equipment. (Wallstreet, 2023)

Like any extreme sports you should have a strong heart for jumping from a high altitude.

103. Go on a Safari

Picture yourself on an African safari, staying at a hotel where giraffes come to poke their head in to say good morning. Instead of guns, the only shots taken at the wildlife you meet are photographs. Safaris are a popular option for tourism in Africa and you can find many versions as you complete your research.

What is a safari ? Why do we go on safaris? These are common questions that arise when someone raises this as an activity idea. The answer is that a safari is not going to the zoo or watching birds in a park. While many people only think of African safaris, a safari refers to experiencing wild life in a natural habitat such as deserts and forests. There are many ways you can enjoy a safari including game watching, small plane rides, boat, or canoe trips and even on foot. Walking through the wild forests or deserts with elephants, giraffes or maybe tigers in your vicinity is how you can feel the excitement through this venture.

African Budget Safari has programs for tourists with safe and promising adventurous tours around the natural habitats of wildlife (Davies, 2022). Africa is known for its safari tours and has the biggest wildlife sanctuary than any other country in the world. There are also safari tours that are organized in Australia, Canada, and even India nowadays.

104. Swim With the Sharks

You can get up close and personal with a variety of shark species, if you are so inclined. Cage diving is the method used where you, as the diver, are enclosed in a steel cage while the sea creatures swim about. It is strongly suggested to keep your limbs in the cage if you want to keep them at all!

This may sound daring and somewhat unimaginable to some but it is actually a sport taken up by many young adults or even older people today. The best and safest option would be the caged dives especially for beginners. There are many good reasons for you to have a wonderful experience in the ocean while observing these majestic creatures. Here are some points for you to consider and reason why you must try to experience this sport:

- Sharks are beautiful and interesting creatures
- You can learn about the ocean habitat and understand how to support aquatic life

- You don't have to be a good swimmer and just have the minimum skill of snorkeling

- Diving with sharks does not cost much

- A good diving team can assist you so you do not need to fear any unexpected attacks

There are many kinds of calm sharks such as whales, blue sharks, nurse sharks, or basking sharks. They are more safe to confront than the aggressive sharks like bull sharks or white sharks. If you are a nature loving and ocean life enthusiast then you can have a great opportunity to come close to underwater life.

Some of the notable sites for swimming with sharks are the Wolf and Darwin islands in Galapagos, Socorro Island and Isla Mujeres in Mexico, the Ningaloo Reef in Western Australia, the Oslob in the Philippines, and Bahia de Los Angeles. In addition to these sites, the best one is the UNESCO World Heritage Site in the Philippines called the Tubbataha Reefs Natural Park. Here you can swim with the amazing whale sharks and is considered to be the best spot to do so (*Swimming With Sharks: Why Would Anyone Do This ?*, n.d.).

105. Participate in an Off-Road Car Rally

For all you car enthusiasts, why not take your skills on the road. There are many options for car rallies on all types of terrain. You can even build up your skills and enter the Dakar rally in Saudi Arabia as an amateur. This grueling event is a one of a kind race over the desert. Sounds like the adult version of playing with Dinky cars and Hot Wheels in the dirt.

Off road car rallies are available in many regions. The terrain can vary depending on your location. The rougher the terrain, the more enjoyable the course will be.

106. Try Ax Throwing

Another relatively new public activity is ax throwing. There are specific venues designed with all the safety features and proper targets where you can try your luck. Axes are provided, so don't worry, you don't have to bring your own, though participants in the competitive stream will have their own personal tools.

This is also a competitive activity, where you can try your luck against an opponent. Each person or team of two tries to score points by throwing their ax at a bullseye, similar to an archery target. The closer your ax sticks to the center, the more points you accumulate.

107. Complete a 5k Marathon

Running is not something many people pick up as a new activity in retirement. Most people have made running a habit for most of their lives. If you enjoy running, why not enter a 5k or 10k race? People of all skill levels can work their way up to being able to complete the race.

Some of the more prestigious events, like the Boston or New York marathons require you to have a minimum qualifying time and pay an entry fee in order to participate. Qualifying times vary by age, then gender within each age group.

108. Try Your Hand at Water Polo

If you enjoy swimming and you are comfortable with your ability to tread water for extended periods, consider trying your hand at water polo. This is a team sport played with a net at each of the "water court," a ball, and a whole lot of attitude. Check with your community pool and swimming clubs to see if there are any recreational water polo events in your area.

109. Take up Boxing

A little sparring in the ring can help keep you fit and relieve stress. There is more to being a pugilist than just throwing punches and a full 10 rounds in the ring can be physically demanding. In the early 1800s, a sports writer in Britain dubbed boxing the "sweet science," due to the planning and strategy required before the first punch is even thrown (Boxrope Team, 2023).

Boxing itself is a low-impact activity which is ideal for seniors with mobility issues. A few lessons and you'll be dancing in the ring with the best of them!. Boxing clubs are accessible in most communities and can provide an opportunity for social activities as well.

110. Test New Heights With a Hot Air Balloon Ride

Imagine floating peacefully over the countryside, watching the sun rise from the basket of your hot air balloon. Although you may have to search for a company in your area that offers this activity, it can be a memorable event. Most balloon rides take place at sunrise, and some offer champagne breakfasts to celebrate the ride. The weather can be a factor in scheduling your ride and you may have to wait for the perfect conditions before taking off.

Hot air balloon rides are fun and adventurous and you cannot be bored on this ride that allows you to get a bird's eye view of the city. Take your minicameras and take some pictures from above but be careful not to drop anything!

Key Takeaways

Chapter 10 has introduced us to some exhilarating

options for fun and adventure. We have reached new heights with hot air ballooning and sunk to the depths in a cage as sharks consider us as an appetizer. There is something for everyone with an adventurous nature.

If there is a sport or risky undertaking you have always wanted to attempt, your retirement is the time to investigate it. Don't live with the thought that you wish you had tried something and didn't. There are many more options than those we have been able to include here, however, these extreme activities will provide a jumping off point. Yes, I said that!

As we move on to our final list of 15 items in the next chapter, we will stay grounded with activities closer to home.

Chapter 11:

All Around Activities Close

to Home

Let's take a look at the list of items that you set aside for "when I retire." We all have that list of activities we have put on the "back burner" for the right moment, when you can devote time to it. That may be binge-watching episodes of a favorite TV series, reading a trilogy from a favorite author, or any number of those "tomorrow" activities.

We have discussed many of priority items such as fitness, travel, education, and expanding your social and spiritual horizons in the previous chapters. Now it is time to look at some of the other activities closer to home that may be less obvious bucket list items, but a great way to enjoy your retirement days.

Here are some items both in the home and in your community that you can do.

111. Find Do-It-Yourself Projects

Do-It-Yourself (DIY) projects have grown in popularity with every age group over the years. Now that you are retired, and have more time to devote to these options, you can set aside the out-of-the-box solutions and dive in.

There are several options in this area of interest such as repairing items, painting furniture, home restoration, and even crafting. There are a variety of resources and tutorials that you can find on the internet for small or big projects. There are online videos and support options through YouTube for even the trickiest projects. However, if you aren't too keen on using online sources, find a book about DIY projects at your local library. The larger hardware and home improvement stores often provide DIY classes, and the staff are eager to help answer all your questions. There are many workshops that will guide you through simple activities such as building furniture, designing decorative shelves, landscaping, and more.

DIY projects help you to keep you engaged and expand your creativity. There is definitely a sense of accomplishment when you complete these activities. You can choose some of the following ideas for DIY projects:

- Build your own entertainment unit: Building a new entertainment center in your living room could help you to organize your little used items that lie around the place. Besides this, your home will be looking a lot different and this new look brings a lot of attention too. Invite your family and friends over for a great movie or game to watch together which will also give a chance to show off your own creation.

- Build wooden shelves for decoration: You could create additional space in your living room by making shelves out of wood for your decorative items or showpieces. Or you can construct floating shelves in your garage for all the nuts and bolts.

- Build a custom bookshelf: A bookshelf is the next best thing you will need to complete your furniture. Books are always a fascination for many who still love to read more than watching TV or the internet.

- Make your own pencil holders: Your pens and pencils may need a proper place to stand so they do not get in the way or get lost among your household items. You can use a wooden log and drill holes in it for holding the pencils. To make it rotate you can use a "lazy Susan," a rotating tool which is used for turntables. Attach the lazy Susan at the bottom so the pencil holder can rotate.

- Organize your closet: You can easily customize your closet with simple tool guides such as from ClosetMaid Selectives or other similar DIY closet systems. This will help you organize clothes and accessories with separate drawers, shelves, and hangers.

- Build an elevated garden bed: Raised garden beds are popular, especially in areas where the ground may flood or small animals can invade your garden. You can make the bed any size, shape, or style you want,

- Create a terrarium: If you are looking to create a home for your amphibian friends, this may be the perfect DIY project. You can make a unique habitat for them to enjoy.

- Make farmhouse-styled furniture: There are lots of options to build furniture as DIY projects. This particular style of furniture may be one that will interest you.

112. Try Out a Video or Virtual Reality Game

Don't let the younger generations have all the fun here. If you haven't tried a virtual reality game, complete with head gear and hand controls, now is the time to do it. There are a lot of different levels to try. Ask your younger family members to assist you. This can be a great way to bridge any generational gaps and find a common ground. Who knows, this could become a new competitive activity for your family. Bragging rights are yours for the taking.

Video games have been evolving amazingly fast nowadays and technology is advancing to such an extent today that in no time people will be working with robots and holograms at work or even at home. You should find this opportunity to spend time to understand this new era of technology and the new techniques that have been introduced into the gaming world. It is always fascinating to learn more about how AI is also taking a role in our information technology or IT industry.

113. Write a How-To Book

In Chapter 5, we discussed side hustles and making extra money in retirement. One of those items, number 56, was *Be a Freelance Writer or Ghost Writer*. In this current chapter, it is time to take your writing skills a step further to write a nonfiction book. If you have a topic that interests you and you have information to share, putting pen to paper and writing a book may be for you.

It does take planning and hard work to get your thoughts organized sufficiently. How-to and self-help books are great sellers, and an opportunity for you to share your thoughts and feelings about your favorite topic. People love to get tried-and-true ideas from other everyday folks. Think about all the books and resources you reach out for when you are looking for a guide. There will be plenty of research involved and reference checking. There are numerous support options to help you on your journey. Start by researching the requirements for book writing and publishing at your local library, book store, or online.

When you choose a topic for your book you should have a good knowledge of what you are writing about. For example, if you were working as a teacher in your earlier years then you write about "how to be the best teacher" or "how to maintain a disciplined classroom." These are just suggestions to lead you towards some great ideas for your topic. The more you know about the topic the more you will have to share with your readers.

114. Digitize Your Picture Albums

I have tons of pictures. Real, hard copy pictures. Masses of picture albums full of these visual memories. I love looking at these albums from time to time, but realistically, most of my newer pictures are on my phone, the computer, or backed up in the cloud. If you are not familiar with that term—the cloud—I would strongly recommend you add an activity to your list to research data storage and backup options, or include it with activity number *69. Enhance Your Technical Knowledge.*

The younger generations don't have a use for—or appreciation of—the old albums, although the pictures themselves are valuable. Scanning your pictures may take a lot of time, but is a worthwhile activity for your retirement. Once you have digitized your pictures, you have more flexibility to keep and share these treasures.

115. Research Your Genealogy/Ancestry

Our next fun idea that you can try at home has something to do with history. Exploring your family history and genealogy is a fulfilling and educational activity for you to try. It is a great way to learn and understand your family's heritage when searching for your ancestral history. You can try online genealogy databases with websites like *Ancestry*, *MyHeritage*, and *FamilySearch*, which offer vast collections of historical records and birth records.

You can also try the local library and archives. You can try the national and state archives as well, which have a lot of historical records, including military service, birth records, death and land records, and even naturalization records.

The great part about finding out where you come from is that you learn about your family roots, what they have experienced, and what remaining family you have out there that you never knew you had. This gives you a great sense of purpose and fulfillment while enjoying the benefits of socialization when you speak to and meet other people.

116. Attend a Comedy Festival

Looking for an opportunity to laugh until your cheeks hurt? Find a local comedy club or check online for a festival in your area. Comedy clubs often have little known comics you can see for low prices. You may have to pay more for some of the well-known comedians, but they do put on quite a show, and are always accompanied by other good comics.

Comedy can be quite subjective, so make sure you research the theme and any disclaimers before attending the show. If you are easily offended by colorful language and uncomfortable subjects, you may want to watch a recording of the artist before you consider purchasing tickets.

117. Take in a Concert

No matter what style of music you like, you can find a concert to attend. Expand your horizons and attend one you might not normally go to. For example, if you haven't attended a rock concert before, search online for artists coming to a venue near you. In the summer, some symphony and jazz groups provide outdoor concerts.

Some music festivals can span a few days to a week. Instead of buying tickets to one show by one artist, you get a pass for the whole day or the complete festival. Camping at one of these events can be an experience. Check for a venue near you and book an event.

118. Attend an Immersive Art Exhibit

Another relatively new style of entertainment are immersive art exhibits. These are expertly-orchestrated digital light shows focusing on the work of a famous artist. Most of the artists are painters, however this presentation method can be used for a multitude of other art types as well. According to Weiner, (22), these animated exhibits draw the spectators in so that you feel one with the images projected. All your senses are tested, as you smell the flowers and feel the fish swimming by. Whatever is projected on the walls around you becomes a full sensory experience.

Two of the most popular exhibits on tour highlight the work of Van Gogh and Dali. Even if you are not necessarily a fan of these artists or their paintings, the opportunity to be part of this digital display and learn more about the life of the artist and their work in this ultra-modern format is memorable.

119. Join a Theatre Group or Make Your Own

If you fancy yourself a bit of an actor, or have always wanted to be part of a theater group, this is your chance. Start with an acting class or two and see where that takes you. There are many small community theater groups that put on shows for the public. These performances can be anything from classic Shakespeare, to an amateur production of any style. This is another good option to socialize during your retirement.

You can always find people with the same interests and even from different age groups who are interested in musicals, cultural acts, or drama. You can find them through community organizations or online and form a group of your own.

Here are some things you can do to start your own group:

- Have a business plan for your company and determine a group name.

- Open a website with the name and details of your company.

- Market your group, focusing on the expertise you bring and events being considered when advertising on social media.

- Add contact information to your site so people can easily reach out to you.

As part of the planning you do for your theater group, fix a budget if you need to have group meetings, get costumes, and provide refreshments for your members. Also, as your group starts to grow you may want to monetize your memberships. You can even use this budget to make flyers to advertise your theater group shows once you become successful.

120. Learn to Knit or Crochet

This is another one of those activities I have heard people say they wish that they had learned. Well, there is no time like the present to learn. Both of these activities are beneficial for relaxation and stress relief. While there are tutorials online, and numerous how-to videos on YouTube, there is nothing like an in-person needlework circle to help you when you are stuck. Knitting and/or crocheting items you have designed yourself can be rewarding and even profitable if you choose to sell your work.

Apart from the creativity and designing skills that you can apply to crocheting there are other benefits from this activity such as:

- engaging your brain and increasing cognitive skills.

- improving self-confidence and self-esteem.

- increasing your social connection by joining a group or knitting club.

- helping reduce stress and manage anxiety.

- improved dexterity which reduces the probability of dropping things (Ellacott, 2023).

Knitting and crocheting are portable activities. You can take them with you wherever you go and work on your craft while waiting for a bus, in a doctor's office or any other location.

121. Attend a Sporting Event

With so many options to choose from, and all the time in the world now, this should be an activity you can easily check off your bucket list. You will have a variety of professional and amateur sports available to you depending on where you live. If you like baseball, see if you can get tickets for a weekend series when your favorite team is playing. Or you can decide to take in multiple events for different sports. Attend an event for a sport that is unfamiliar to you, like show jumping (horses) or jai alai. If you have the opportunity, why not take in some Olympic events or trials?

There are many community sport events that take place in your area or neighboring clubs which you can attend alone or with a friend. When attending an event with a friend it gives you more satisfaction sharing the activity. Local sports teams welcome the audience, which provides them the motivation to do their best. While attending professional sports events can become quite costly, amateur sports can be equally entertaining for a fraction of the cost.

122. Build a Greenhouse

If you are looking for a new adventure to further test your green thumb, why not build a greenhouse on your property. This is a great option for anyone living in a climate where the growing season may be short and you may be limited with the variety of items you can grow outside.

Greenhouse gardening will give you the option to try growing fruits, vegetables, or plants that may not thrive outdoors. You can find a variety of styles, sizes, and floor plans online, as well as methods for irrigation and venting. If you have limited space in your property, there are options for lean-to greenhouses, which use one of the walls of your house as a side of the structure.

When planning to start your own greenhouse make sure you make a list of the items and resources you need as well as the place you want to set it on. There are so many options of plants, herbs, fruits, or vegetables to grow in your own self-made greenhouse. You can choose a variety of flowers by planting seeds in rows or columns that will give a decorative look. Your family and neighbors would love to come and admire your creations and might even follow you. So, you are not only building a natural ecosystem but also help keeping a healthy environment as well.

123. Spoil Your Grandchildren

Here is an activity that will make you smile just thinking about time with your grandchildren or other young ones in your family. While we were working regularly, it was tough to squeeze in the time we wanted to be able to spoil the young ones. With more time available during your retirement, you will have the opportunities to participate in their lives and shower them with all the love, affection, and treats imaginable.

Your grandchildren are always eager to share their favorite games and hobbies with you. They enjoy any opportunity to share their latest achievements with their dearest grandma or granddad. Choose a time when your grandchildren could come to visit or you can visit them yourselves and spend some quality time with them while they are young.

124. Start a Band or Acapella Group

What a great opportunity to start a musical group. If you already have the talent within your social circle you have a head start. Otherwise, you can reach out to your local community or senior center to see if there are any other like-minded individuals around.

If you do get a band or acapella group together there will always be options to display your talent. Many bars and restaurants will jump at the opportunity to have live talent at their establishment, especially if you are going to bring in family and friends as customers.

There is still the opportunity to learn something before you start your own group of musicians. Find out who has talents in playing any musical instrument and possibly you might even gather a group who can play together. You never know you might become famous as a senior group and find some good followers.

125. Visit Museums and Art Galleries

Did you know that you could visit your local museums and art galleries virtually? This way, you don't have to travel through wet or cold weather to enjoy some culture. You can enjoy art and history from the comfort of your own home!

Go online and discover different virtual events or special time-limited exhibits. For example, an Egyptian themed exhibit with mummies and other period artifacts is often on tour, stopping in at designated museums around the world. Find out which are available and come to a museum near you. Or find out if there is a virtual tour option for the exhibit, where you can attend online. Do note that most of these exhibits will charge a fee, but the memories made are worth it.

Key Takeaways

This chapter introduced the final fifteen options as we reached our 125 activities. We looked at activities you can attend, such as concerts, festivals, and exhibits, as well fun things you can do, such as research your ancestry or write a book.

This is by no means the end though. In fact, my hope is that you will use this book and the recommended activities listed to trigger your imagination. In our final chapter, I'll speak to the ways you can use the fun and adventurous activities we've discussed as a starting point for your retirement roadmap.

Chapter 12:

What's on Your Bucket

List?

Now that you have had a look at the 125 fun and adventurous activities in this book, I'm sure your wheels are turning, thinking of so many other items you can add. There are options to build on each of the activities named. Consider variations with the number of people, the location, and the time you want to invest. Develop a healthy outlook and explore spiritualization, and mental and physical well-being as you progress through your newfound freedom in retirement. You can come up with your own list of activities that you would like to try out. Jot them down and check them off as you try each one.

Even something like drafting or updating your will can be an adventure. I bet you are asking how drafting your will could be considered a fun, adventurous activity. Believe me, you will be smiling once you have completed it, more so with relief than anything else. There are a number of online legal will programs that have standard forms and selections you can customize for your needs.

If you already have a will, now is the chance to take the time and update it if needed. Make sure you have a power of attorney and living wills created as well, so that your wishes are documented. Having these forms completed online allows you to update and change the options as different life events occur. This is also a great time to revisit your assets, see if any of them—or the designated recipient—are no longer valid.

Don't be afraid to consider all your senses when you are looking for activities. Much of the information presented in this book focuses on things you see. Like the information on culinary choices, think about other ways you can tantalize your taste buds. What are some of the ways you can test your sense of smell, hearing, and touch. Thinking of activities that hit all your senses can open up more opportunities for you.

Have you ever seen the old 2007 movie *The Bucket List*, starring Morgan Freeman and Jack Nicholson? This is when the common term was promoted. After this movie, many people walked around talking about the weird and wonderful adventures they always wanted to do but never have. Sometimes, we wait too long to achieve those special adventures.

Here are some additional ideas that can give you inspiration for what to include in your bucket list:

- Take up a new seasonal sport

- Invest in crypto currency

- Binge watch every episode of a popular TV show or series

- Redecorate your house

- Sell your house

- Clean out the basement and attic. Hold a yard sale and donate the proceeds to charity

- Climb a mountain

Set goals for yourself. See how much you can explore and discover. Do it on your own, with your partner, as part of a group, or even with a buddy to keep you company and share the experiences. Make the world a fun and engaging place by taking advantage of all it has to offer. You are the one making the path to your destination, so try out all you've ever dreamed of experiencing.

There is so much to do. You are only limited by your dreams, wishes, and imagination. Be inspired; come up with your own list of items that will bring you joy and make the most of your retirement days!

The lines below can be used to record your ideas. If you run out of space, and your own lines, use post-it notes, or any method you choose to keep expanding your list

Conclusion

Just because you've finally retired doesn't mean that the only thing you can do is sit back on your couch and watch TV. Life can be far more fulfilling. The world has an endless amount of fun opportunities and activities for you to try out. It's up to you to get out there, give it a shot, and try all of the things that you have always dreamed of doing.

Hopefully, *125 Fun Things to Do in Retirement* has shown us that there are so many different types of activities; more than we ever imagined. And this is just the tip of the iceberg. As mentioned in the introduction, this is a roadmap for you to start your journey. You can keep yourself occupied with more than just one type of activity, and there are endless benefits that come from each and every option. We have barely scratched the surface with the material in this book.

It is called a bucket list because you have the opportunity to gather resources and contain them in this central location, ready for the picking. You could even have a completed bucket and another as a "to do" bucket. Share the completed items with members of your social circle and see if this triggers any new suggestions.

It doesn't matter what type of personality you have; there are adventures out there for everyone to try. Now you have the time to devote to investigating all of the experiences waiting for you. Not having the time is no longer a valid excuse. You don't have the money? Check out the items in Chapter 4 for suggestions to make some extra money, then go ahead and complete that pending activity. Have you always wanted to learn a musical instrument or a new skill? Have you always wanted to find a way to connect with your deeper and spiritual self? Have you always wanted to see the Swiss Alps or take a gondola ride in Venice? Well, now is the time for you to go out there and make all of your dreams come true. Now it's time for you to explore the world, travel the seven seas, go treasure hunting, and so much more.

You have the power and the control to take the reins and do what makes you happy. Make sure that you are keeping yourself fit, healthy, and excited about every day that comes. You don't have to spend your time depressed and wondering about what is beyond the four walls around you. Now is the time to go out to explore the world, find out who you are, and reach all of those dreams you set for yourself years ago. So what are you waiting for? Start filling out that bucket list with ideas and start ticking them off. So go for it, my dear retiree!

Live your life to the fullest. Embrace all the adventures and cherish the laughter as you revel in the freedom of not working. Your retirement awaits, and the possibilities that you have yet to encounter are endless. Cheers to an extraordinary retirement filled with joy, fulfillment, and the knowledge that all your wildest dreams will come true!

If you have found this book helpful for your retirement planning and it stimulated your creative side, please leave a review for other retirees who may need a prod to get them off the couch. Thank you!

Scan QR Code with your phone to leave a review or just press the star rating. Thank you!

http://www.amazon.com/review/create-review?&asin=B0CLHNBD9J

About the Author

Pam Martin has a deep-seated desire for adventure and loves communing with nature. After many years of the tedious 9-5 and mini-excursion vacations, she decided to "retire" earlier than planned to pursue a one-year epic trip across the United States exploring the natural wonders of all the National Parks with full intentions of going back to work afterwards. At the end of the trip, she discovered she had replaced her days of pressure and dreaded deadlines with the more pleasing pursuits of being a self-made travel agent. Pam's next exciting destinations involve her passion as a novice history buff, a treasurer hunter of geocaching, admirer of awesome sunsets, and lover of waterfalls in various settings.

Married for over 45 years, Mike and Pam have three children and 11 grandchildren. They live in the Asheville, NC area and continue to travel in their RV motorhome, fulfilling the next destination of adventure and exploration. Pam enjoys traveling, geocaching, hiking, reading, writing, and working on various small business endeavors to keep the juices flowing.

Appendix 1:

125 Activities List

1. Walk the Block

2. Try Tai Chi

3. Become Flexible With Yoga

4. Dance for Fun and Exercise

5. Hit the Golf Course

6. Go Fishing

7. Play Tennis

8. Take Up Table Tennis

9. Play Pickleball

10. Hit the Badminton Birdie

11. Get a Strike at the Bowling Alley

12. Play Bocce Ball

13. Join a Volleyball Team

14. Take Up Archery

15. Go Swimming

16. Reconnect With Friends and Family

17. Join a Local Club or Group

18. Create or Revisit Your Social Media Profile

19. Attend Events That Interest You

20. Join or Create a Community Garden

21. Host a Theme Dinner

22. Attend Card Nights or Game Events

23. Explore Opportunities at Senior Centers and Community Centers

24. Participate in a LARP

25. Join a Fitness Club or Gym

26. Plan a Trip

27. Book a Cruise

28. Rent (or buy) a Recreation Vehicle (RV)

29. Use Your Travel Points

30. Take the Train

31. Go Solo

32. Take a Road Trip

33. Pin the Point on a Map

34. Theme Travel

35. Multiple Transportation Travel

36. Try Your Hand at Photography

37. Take Up Painting

38. Discover Geocaching

39. Complete Furniture or Home Restorations

40. Study Classic Cars

41. Dig Into Gardening

42. Put Pen to Paper and Write

43. Take up Woodworking

44. Grab the Binoculars and Go Bird-Watching

45. Try Music and Musical Instruments

46. Become a Board Game Guru

47. Read for Pleasure

48. Lend a Hand to Environmental Cleanup Projects

49. Test Your Patience With Origami

50. Sell Your Art and Crafts

51. Start a Business

52. Earn Through Passive Income

53. Sell Produce From Your Garden

54. Do Odd Jobs While you Travel

55. House or Pet Sit

56. Become a Handy Person

57. Be a Freelance Writer or Ghost Writer

58. Review Books for Cash

59. Teach a Course

60. Drive for a Ride-Share Service

61. Learn a New Skill

62. Complete a Degree

63. Learn a New Language or Two

64. Take Classes That Interest You

65. Join a Book Club

66. Attend Workshops and Conferences

67. Engage in Brain Training Activities

68. Volunteer in Educational Settings

69. Explore Online Webinars, Podcasts, and TED Talks

70. Enhance Your Technical Knowledge

71. Cultivate Gratitude and Positive Thinking

72. Explore Your Spiritual Self

73. Try Meditation Training

74. Engage in Mindfulness Practices

75. Join a Bible Study Group

76. Take Religious Classes or Workshops

77. Participate in Personal Development Courses

78. Attend a Wellness Retreat

79. Learn About Blue Zones: Lessons in Longevity

80. Create a Gratitude Calendar

81. Mentor Others

82. Feed the Hungry and Homeless

83. Donate Produce From Your Garden

84. Organize a Fundraiser

85. Foster Rescue Animals

86. Serve on a Non-Profit Board

87. Help with Disaster Relief Efforts

88. Volunteer at a Hospital or Nursing Home

89. Take Your Professional Skill Overseas

90. Read to Elementary School Children

91. Try Different Cultural Restaurants

92. Attempt Climate-Friendly and Sustainable Eating

93. Test Vegan or Plant-Based Nutrition

94. Test Online Nutrition Counseling

95. Try Community Cooking Classes

96. Investigate Cooking for One Options

97. Test Different Takeout Options

98. Host or Attend a Potluck

99. Take a Wine or Beer Tour

100. Eat Crickets

101. Skydiving

102. Try Bungee Jumping Over a Gorge

103. Go on a Safari

104. Swim With the Sharks

105. Participate in an Off Road Car Rally

106. Try Ax Throwing

107. Complete a 5k Marathon

108. Try Your Hand at Water Polo

109. Take up Boxing

110. Test New Heights With a Hot Air Balloon Ride

111. Find Do-It-Yourself Projects

112. Try Out a Video or Virtual Reality Game

113. Write a How-To Book

114. Digitize Your Picture Albums

115. Research Your Genealogy/Ancestry

116. Attend a Comedy Festival

117. Take in a Concert

118. Attend an Immersive Art Exhibit

119. Join a Theatre Group or Make Your Own

120. Learn to Knit or Crochet

121. Attend a Sporting Event

122. Build a Greenhouse

123. Spoil Your Grandchildren

124. Start a Band or Acapella Group

125. Visit Museums and Art Galleries

References

American Association of Retired Persons. (n.d.). Job
    Accommodation Network.
    https://askjan.org/organizations/American-
    Association-of-Retired-
    Persons.cfm#:~:text=About%3A,through%20i
    nformation%2C%20advocacy%20and%20servi
    ce.

Ashford, K. (2023, January 4). 6 ways to make extra
    money in retirement.
    https://www.nerdwallet.com/article/finance/e
    xtra-money-retirement

Bonnenberg, B. J., Dube, J.-P., & Joo, J. (2021, April 1).
    Millennials and the Take-Off of Craft Brands:
    Preference Formation in the US Beer Industry.
    BFI. https://bfi.uchicago.edu/insight/research-
    summary/millennials-and-the-take-off-of-craft-
    brands-preference-formation-in-the-us-beer-
    industry/

Boxrope Team. (2023, June 13). Why Is Boxing Called
    "The Sweet Science"? BOXROPE®.
    https://boxrope.com/en-
    ca/blogs/boxing/why-is-boxing-called-the-
    sweet-science

Candy Stripers: A Journey of Hospital Volunteers in the United States. (2023, June 24). Www.volunteerfdip.org. https://www.volunteerfdip.org/a-journey-of-hospital-volunteers-in-united-states

Cheal, D. (2022). Trans-Europe Express. https://ig.ft.com/life-of-a-song/trans-europe-express.html#:~:text=In%201977%2C%20Kraftwerk%20brought%20trains,a%20new%20borderless%20postwar%20continent.

Crow, S., & Weisman, C. (2023, June 29). *50 easy DIY projects you can tackle this weekend*. Best life online. https://bestlifeonline.com/easy-diy-home-projects/

Davies, L. (2022, May 6). What is Safari ? Wildlife safari in Africa. African budget safaris. https://www.africanbudgetsafaris.com/blog/what-is-a-safari/#:~:text=In%20summary%2C%20a%20safari%20is,East%20Africa%20and%20Southern%20Africa

Disaster relief services. (2023). American Red Cross. https://www.redcross.org/about-us/our-work/disaster-relief.html

Ellacott, S. (2023, January 29). *5 reasons knitting and crochet are good for your health*. (2023, January 29). Knit happens. https://knit-happens.co.uk/5-

reasons-knitting-crochet-are-good-for-your-health/#:~:text=Knitting%20and%20crochet%20involve%20complex,decline%2C%20especially%20in%20older%20adults.

5 tips for sustainable eating: The nutrition source. (2023). Harvard T.H. Chan. https://www.hsph.harvard.edu/nutritionsource/2015/06/17/5-tips-for-sustainable-eating/

Fun activities for seniors: Over 100 ways to play. (2022, April 22). Great senior living. https://www.greatseniorliving.com/articles/fun-activities-for-seniors#learning

Georgetown Home Care. (2020, July 19). 10 Ways to Keep Seniors Active. Georgetown Home Care. https://www.georgetownhomecare.com/10-creative-ideas-to-keep-seniors-active/

Gratitude calendar to boost your mental health and optimize performance. (2022, September 26). HPRC. https://www.hprc-online.org/mental-fitness/spiritual-fitness/gratitude-calendar#:~:text=Use%20HPRC's%20gratitude%20calendar%20to,experience%20more%20good%20each%20day.

How to start a theater company. (2023, May 12). How to start an LLC.

https://howtostartanllc.com/business-ideas/theatre-company

Lopaz, K. (2018, May 13). 5 top part-time jobs for retired seniors who need some extra cash. USA Today. https://www.usatoday.com/story/money/careers/part-time-careers/2018/05/13/5-top-part-time-jobs-for-retired-seniors-who-need-some-extra-cash/34546735/

Mccarthy, I. (2021, January 5). What's Bugging You? 10 of the Best Insect Delicacies Around the World. Www.finedininglovers.com. https://www.finedininglovers.com/article/insect-delicacies-around-world

Merriam-Webster. (n.d.). Mindfulness. In Merriam-Webster.com dictionary. Retrieved July 19, 2023, from https://www.merriam-webster.com/dictionary/mindfulness

Oil-free vegan recipes- The simple veganista. (n.d.). Simple-veganista. https://simple-veganista.com/recipes/diet/oil-free/

Planning a successful fundraising event in 10 steps. (2023). Onecause. https://www.onecause.com/blog/fundraising-event-planning/#goals

Plant-based diet recipes. (n.d.). BBC Good Food. https://www.bbcgoodfood.com/recipes/collec tion/plant-based-diet-recipes

Sauer, A. (2023). Benefits of traveling later in life. Leisure care. https://www.leisurecare.com/resources/benefit s-senior- travel/#:~:text=Travel%20abroad%20can%20 make%20the,out%20of%20their%20comfort% 20zone.

Sennebogen, E., & Jaracz, J. (n.d.). 10 tips for restoring old furniture. https://home.howstuffworks.com/home- improvement/home-diy/projects/5-tips-for- restoring-old-furniture.htm

Skydiving Age Limit: Can you be too old? (2016). Wisconsin Skydiving Center. https://wisconsinskydivingcenter.com/blog/sk ydiving-age-limit-too-old-to-skydive/

Stanko, C. (2023, August 4). *15-minute potluck ideas that'll feed a crowd.* Taste of Home. https://www.tasteofhome.com/collection/15- minute-potluck-ideas/15-minute

Swimming with sharks: Why would anyone do this? (n.d.). A- Z-Animals. https://a-z- animals.com/blog/swimming-with-sharks-why-would-anyone-do-this/#:~:text=It%20is%20Safe%20to%20Swim%20with%20Sharks&text=Even%20when%20diving%20with%20more,if%20you%20swim%20with%20them.

Tips from people who started a business after retiring. (n.d.). Huntington. https://www.huntington.com/learn/invest-retire/starting-a-business-after-retirement

Train Travel In Europe. (n.d.). https://www.seat61.com/european-train-travel.htm#:~:text=There's%20no%20need%20to%20fly,and%20where%20to%20buy%20tickets.

Valera, S. (2023, May 12). Best online nutrition counseling programs. Very well fit. https://www.verywellfit.com/best-online-nutrition-counseling-programs-5073716

Volunteer opportunities- Senior services. (2023). Atlantic Health. https://www.atlantichealth.org/conditions-treatments/senior-services/volunteer-opportunities.html

Wallstreet, B. (2023. March 2). *How dangerous is bungee jumping ?* Cavern Tours. https://caverntours.com/how-dangerous-is-

bungee-jumping/#:~:text=The%20majority%20of%20
bungee%20operations,with%20a%20stellar%20
safety%20record.

Weiner, A. (2022, February 10). *The Rise of "Immersive" Art*. The New Yorker. https://www.newyorker.com/news/letter-from-silicon-valley/the-rise-and-rise-of-immersive-art

What is continuing education ? (2021, January 19). Settlement. https://settlement.org/ontario/education/adult-education/what-is-adult-education/what-is-continuing-education-/

What is nutrition counseling ? And how does it help seniors ? (2023, February 7). National Council on Aging. https://www.ncoa.org/article/what-is-nutrition-counseling-is-it-right-for-me

Made in United States
Troutdale, OR
10/10/2024

23634201R10089